T0194929

DOING THIS LIFE THING TOGETHER

MARQUITA L. DANZY AND NIYA S. DANZY

WESTBOW
PRESS®
A DIVISION OF THOMAS NELSON
& ZONDERVAN

Scripture quotations are from the ESV® Bible (The Holy Bible, English Standard Version®), copyright © 2001 by Crossway, a publishing ministry of Good News Publishers. Used by permission. All rights reserved.

WestBow Press books may be ordered through booksellers or by contacting:

WestBow Press
A Division of Thomas Nelson & Zondervan
1663 Liberty Drive
Bloomington, IN 47403
www.westbowpress.com
1 (866) 928-1240

ISBN: 978-1-9736-1175-2 (sc)
ISBN: 978-1-9736-1176-9 (hc)
ISBN: 978-1-9736-1174-5 (e)

Library of Congress Control Number: 2017919439

Print information available on the last page.

WestBow Press rev. date: 01/17/2018

Dedication

To my mother, Pastor Iola Danzy, (aka, Mom Dukes):

As long as I'm alive, you'll never want for shrimp again.
You are loved and adored by your children and your grandchildren.
Thank you for every sacrifice that you've made for us.

To everyone that has contributed to our lives in any way,

Thank you.

Freedom begins when you make a conscious decision
to finally live; live in liberty.

When you stare yourself in the eyes and decree
"I'll be exactly who God created me to be."

When the review of your past and the preview of your
future meet, and you treat them both the same.

Proud of where you're going and from whence you came.
Oh, when you allow God to fortify your inner man
where you finally understand the plans He has for you.

When you embrace destiny like your long-lost friend, freedom begins.
When you love yourself enough to begin again, freedom begins.

When the ifs and whens, the they and thems, the
should-haves and could-haves begin to make you mad enough
to change. Yeah, it may sound strange but you're on your way.

When faults no longer define you, failure no longer
blinds you, fear no longer confines you.

When a box cannot contain you, pain cannot restrain you,
and regret loses power to retain you.

You my friend are free, free to be, free like me.

Let's go!

Free Spoken Word
From the EP *Free* by MarQuita L. Danzy

The *Free* EP and single **You Get the Glory** by MarQuita L. Danzy
are available for download on all digital outlets.

Contents

Foreword

Being a parent is one of the most fulfilling jobs a person can have. As Christian parents, we have the unique opportunity to make an eternal investment in the lives of our children. However, children don't come with a set of instructions or guide book. Consequently, there seems be a lot of guess work involved with child-rearing.

In the last few decades, society has strayed away from the importance that parenting holds. We have seen the family redefined so much that, in many cases, the parent-child relationship is seemingly non-existent. Parenting is fading away, and, with it, we are losing God's blessing and missing the mark.

Becoming a good parent is not automatic - it takes time and effort. We must be willing to invest in this most important task. A parent should present the fundamental qualities of leadership, responsibility, and accountability, as well as the capabilities of planning, disciplining, and loving. Parenting is a full-time job.

In their book, MarQuita and Niya provide a fresh look at the parent-child relationship and its challenges. They share stories and principles from their lives for effective 21st century parenting.

They share the roles, vision, relationship, management, and communication skills of their parent-child relationship structure. They share prayers and Scriptures to apply to daily living. Their tips in each chapter challenge you to explore fresh alternatives and innovative concepts to assist and enhance your parent-child relationship structure.

In a time when there are growing gaps, we need books with practical steps and insights. We need more good parent-child relationships. This book is an invaluable tool that will indeed help meet that need.

LaMont Turner

1

So, What Is This About?

MarQuita: ★Walks towards the front door to answer★ Hey! How are you? We've been awaiting your arrival. Niya, say hello to our guest!

Niya: ★With a straight face void of expression★ Hi.

MarQuita: ★Shaking my head at Niya but turning my attention back to you★ Come on in. We are honored that you are here with us. Are you comfortable? Good.

Let's chat about life - the greatest gift given to each spirit by God the Creator to become a soul; a soul with a divine purpose to fulfill within a set time on this earth. As it journeys towards its purpose, the soul is granted the opportunity to experience many things. Among these are love and laughter, joy and pain, heartbreak and healing. The route is charted by our heavenly Father. Our decisions can alter it. Time is the invisible yet ever present companion of life. It moves forward regardless. The wise soul embraces this reality wholeheartedly and attempts to move with (and within) time recognizing that this journey, despite the actual number of chronological days given, is swift; so swift that they must take every opportunity to make the best of it (whatever that means).

Niya: Speaking of time...how long is this going to take? I have plans.

MarQuita: *I'm sorry? Where do you have to go? No ma'am. Have a seat and join us. Now, where was I? Oh yes! I remember. Life's journey!*

Impersonates train conductor "Next stop, Motherhood" did not come at what I would have considered the greatest time for me. You see, I had this list and it was organized. My goals were set in the order in which I wanted to accomplish them. High school? Check! Undergraduate degree? Check! Post graduate degree? Check! Return home after being away for so many years? Check! Start your career? Check! Everything was going as planned. Naturally, marriage was the next item on my list of things to do however; procreating (which unexpectedly made its way to the top of the list) was far in the distance; somewhere around number 1,250. Simple subtraction makes it safe to conclude that there were 1,249 other things that I wanted to accomplish before I became a mother but here I am, going to be a mother. *Help Wanted!* An instruction manual on how to navigate through the ups and downs, ins and outs, blessings, bumps and bruises, the good, bad, and the unfortunately ugly of this thing called life for me and A BABY! This cannot be happening. Who told God to give *me* a baby? Seriously, where's the instruction manual? Does such a thing exist? Where can I find it? How much does it cost? Who wrote it and what is their experience on the topic? ***Deep sigh***

With so many unanswered questions the one thing that I became absolutely sure of was that my life will never be all about me ever again. From this moment forward, I will have to be the safe and dependable one with all of the answers (until my child realizes that no one has all of the answers). I'll have to be the one they depend on to make things right and keep things together. I'll have to rely on the supernatural insight that comes along with good effective parenting. I'll experience sacrifice on a different level. My prayer life will have to skyrocket. Let me prepare for it now. I'll pray, and then I'll pray again. I'll pray without ceasing. I'll pray in stammering lips with words that cannot be understood by the natural ear! LOL! I'll have to learn how to lean on God for all of the answers when it comes to raising the child that I was given. I'll have to consciously decide on those things (naturally and spiritually) that I want to pass down from my parents and those things that I do not and will not pass down. Oh! The pressure of it all!

Niya: *Clears throat to interject* Let's talk about passing things down. Grandma makes me breakfast, lunch and dinner whenever I stay with her. I'm sure she taught you to do that for me but you don't, so it's like you're not passing that down. You should mom. You should pass that down.

MarQuita: * Stares. Continues*

I was scared. I was scared that I had disappointed my mother. I was scared of what people would say, and scared of how I would react to what people would say. I was most scared of how people would view and treat my child. I always envisioned a celebration with my husband, family and close friends. I never thought I'd have to figure out how to "break the news" to everyone and help them adjust to my new normal. I finally decided to share my fears with my mom. She instantly eased my spirit. My mother told me that this baby was mine, that I had to get myself together and raise him or her, and reassured me that I was surrounded by love. She also told me that she was not babysitting! (That's another story for another day). LOL! The dust began to settle and I began to breathe; that is until another reality hit me like a ton of bricks.

Impersonates train conductor again because I know you thoroughly enjoyed it the first time "Next stop, Single Parenthood." Hold on! Give me a minute here! I'm just getting to a place of accepting that a baby is on the way. I was so concerned about the aforementioned that it took a minute for me to realize that I'm actually going to do all of this without a husband! There's going to be different last names on the birth certificate because we are not married. When the baby starts to cry there will be no supportive kiss on my cheek in the middle of the night coupled with "MarQuita you sleep. It's my turn. I've got it." What a responsibility! I'm not ready. Am I? I don't know how to do this! Or do I? Ok. I'll just make the best of it. How do you attempt to ease the anxiety of motherhood by simply making the best of it? God? Are you there? It's me, MarQuita.

Niya: *Begins to sing a line from one of her favorite Broadway shows* *"Are you there God? It's me..."*

MarQuita: *Cuts eyes at Niya but secretly laughs inside.*

This was rough. Most days my thoughts and emotions were riddled with disappointment and guilt until the day that hope entered the picture. Something inside of me just clicked. From that moment on I decided to be the best mother ever! I decided to work hard so that my child will want for nothing; I mean not one thing. I decided to enjoy the process and celebrate the gift. My heart began to smile. I'm going to be a mother! ***Screams at the top of my lungs*** HEY WORLD, I'M GOING TO BE A MOTHER!

Niya: *Mocks in baby voice* *"I'm going to be a mother."* ***Laughs.***

MarQuita: * Speaks to Niya* *Whatever! This was the moment where it all turned in your favor! You should send up a praise right here!*

Niya: *Stares*

There was no time for a pity party. Sorry misery, I reject your invitation. I cannot be your company! I had to get myself together quickly. God had given me (as He gives all parents) an important task. I must prepare my child for her journey and I have no time to waste. I determined from the very beginning that I will make Niya an active partner in my life. I'm clear. She will not be my equal. I will forever be mom. She will respect me as such. I am more clear that at some point the dynamic of our relationship will change from my being the ultimate decision maker and the one she has to listen to, to my only being the advice giver and the one she can choose to listen to or not.

Niya: *Yeahhhhhh!*

MarQuita: You're excited about having that choice, huh? Bless your heart and all your parts.

I began to pray for wisdom. How I handle Niya in the season of having "the rule over her" will dictate the outcome of our relationship when I have none. I cannot "lord" over a grown person, and I do not want to so I determined to lay the foundation in our home that my child and I will talk openly about any and everything. We will cry and laugh, agree and disagree, teach and learn, explore and travel, rise and fall as long as our souls' journeys allow, and we will do it together. We will not leave each other behind. I will not damage her in order to prove to her that I have authority. She will already know and understand the depth of my authority because I'll walk it out with her. There is no need for competition between us. We do not have to experience the "big I" and "little you" moments. We do not have to fight for the ability to grow. I will not place her in a position to follow me blindly. Why should I? She truly is the only person in this world that knows me from the inside out. I carried her. My blood is running through her veins. She was exposed to everything that I was and will be before I gave her a name. We are forever connected. I am forever hers.

Niya: ⋆Leans over in an attempt to whisper to me⋆ That's sweet Mom. Question: Are there any snacks?

MarQuita: Simone! Go look in my purse and leave me alone. We're trying to have a serious conversation here!

Niya: ⋆Quickly reaches for purse and begins active search⋆

Everything that I will do as her parent will ultimately prepare her to leave me. One day she will make her list and be on her way to follow her dreams and aspirations. Initially, I will have the responsibility and the privilege to have a front row seat as she, in time, experiences all that life has to offer; but one day, I'll have to start taking a back seat. One day I will not physically be here anymore. **⋆Deep sigh.⋆** I cry every time I think about it. I cannot imagine not being around to love, protect and guide her. I cannot imagine not being able to kiss the apples of her cheeks (one of my absolute favorite things to do), hear her voice, her laugh, or see her smile. One day (I hope it's a long, long time from now), she will have to remember me, what I've given her and live on.

Niya: *Looks at mom with sad puppy dog eyes.*

MarQuita: *Looks at Niya with tears in my eyes* I'm sorry love. I know.

At 15 and 41 (we were actually 13 and 39 when we began the process of writing this book); we are at a peculiar place. Niya is the princess of the wonderful world of the teenager, and I am working 41 in a more excellent way! So far, we've survived everything from diapers to potty training, breastfeeding to table food, first words to high school, employment and unemployment, failed relationships and new relationships, from boys are yucky to boys are at least human to boys are **CUTE**, success and failures, life and death – and we still have a long way to go.

It's so amazing that God destined for us to write this book. Our relationship inspires people everywhere that we go. From the gym to the movie theatre, in the states and on other continents, in person and through social media, people are genuinely amazed at our connection. They want to know more about our journey, proving to us that writing this book is NECESSARY. It has truly been a joy to witness my daughter's growth in every way imaginable. She is the absolute love of my life.

Niya: Aweeeeeeee!

The book that you now hold is our story. It is designed to give insight on how we are "doing this life thing together." The topics that we've selected to share are those most prevalent in our lives at this moment in time. Training up a child in the way they should go is all inclusive. The command includes more than just spiritual principles, but ways to successfully handle practical, everyday life situations. We will speak freely and candidly about our feelings, thoughts and actions (positive or negative), what we've learned from living through these topics, and what we are striving to change or perfect moving forward. You will read both of our views on each topic. Immediately following each chapter, we will highlight the points that we believe you cannot afford to miss, share additional insight, tips, or better yet suggestions on what can assist you in reaching maximum success in each area (**"This is how we do it"**).

We end in chapter-specific prayers. Throughout the book, you'll see the highlighted italicized acronym *SWNM* **(Say What Now Moment)**. It is used when the co-writer interjects her thoughts or responses in the midst of the other writer's moment in the book because she just could not conceal it! (You've experienced this already throughout this chapter.)

While reading, please understand that this book is not designed to override your spiritual conviction. As a believer and as an heir of Christ, you have the obligation and authority to go to God and receive insight on what He wants for your life specifically. The views we express are based on our experiences of doing just that. We write with pure intentions, wanting to please God and complete this assignment. We want nothing more than for Him to be glorified. We write with sincere hearts and a sincere love for others. The assignment causes us to be vulnerable. It causes us to speak the truth.

Niya and I are in no way perfect, but that's what makes this so perfect. So, welcome! Welcome to our journey. We are simple God-fearing people. We love hard, play hard, work hard, we laugh even harder, and we chase after the will of God for our lives. We are both growing and relearning ourselves and each other every day. We are learning how to celebrate our similarities as well as our differences. Together we are conquering fears, and challenging ourselves to create lasting memories as we seize every God-ordained opportunity given to us. Our prayer is that our journey helps to build bridges in distant or struggling relationships. We pray that it gives insight for those planning on starting a family. We hope it plants seeds of hope within parent/child relationships. We pray that it gives strength to anyone feeling that they are the only ones experiencing life. We pray that it makes you laugh! We pray that your relationship with God is fortified. As we share our testimony, we pray that you will overcome.

Niya: *That's deep.*

MarQuita: *Well thank you! I can be a little deep at times. LOL!*

Lastly, it is important for me to ask parents to process this book <u>with</u> your child. We strongly believe that readers will not be able to truly understand why we do what we do (the chapters to come) without being given an insider to some of the major stops along our journey, how those stops affected us, and without understanding where I was holistically when my daughter's life began. God has been overly gracious to us. Please stress to your child that God has mercy on whom He will. Teach them that they should never use another person's testimony as permission to test the waters or as an excuse to live however they want to live. They may not survive to tell the story.

Repentance does not save any of us from the repercussions of our actions. I've processed my life with my child in hopes that she will not only see value in the good things that I've done and use them as encouragement to become better in her own journey, but I've also processed my life with her so she can prayerfully avoid the pitfalls that I jumped into. Part of my prayers for her conception to present day is, "Dear God, please do not allow Niya to make any of the mistakes that I've made or anything worse." I have not in the past and will refuse in the present to allow shame to silence me. Sharing is necessary. Ask God for wisdom to know what to share with your children and when. They'll appreciate you and respect you more, and you, you just may save their lives.

Niya: *Yup! What she said.* **★Still searching for snacks.★**

We love you! XO!

2

Here's the Tea!

MarQuita

The year: 2001. The situation: I'm pregnant! I know you're asking how'd that happen, right? Right. Although I could honestly give you a three-word answer (I had sex), I think you deserve more of an engaging conversation, so here's a little tea (history).

In chapter one, we started our conversation about life and the soul's journey. Well, life was quite a journey for my soul at a very young age. I was blessed with a mother who worked amazingly hard as a single parent to provide whatever was needed for my brother and I, a father (who I absolutely adored) who was present and supportive, and a solid educational and spiritual foundation. Our home was safe and thriving. Our village was strong. Our Grandmother Spencer, aunts and uncles along with our cousins helped to care for us. I have fun-filled memories of fantastic family vacations, cookouts, dinners, and the like. My Godmother, Sylvia Holland, was amazing. She kept me close to her. She introduced me to sewing machines and took me to places that sparked my creativity at a young age. All of my friends were "church kids" with a few sprinkled here and there from the neighborhood and school.

God graced me with many spiritual gifts and talents, as well as natural abilities. He also graced me with a pastor at that time who encouraged the operation of my gifts and allowed them to mature within me so much so that, as a child, I worked hard as a leader within the ministry. I was an honor roll student spending countless hours studying to pass tests, practicing instruments, arranging songs, planning rehearsals and studying scripture in order to teach Sunday school at church while still attending a series of extracurricular activities designed to shape me into the wonderful woman with poise and class that you see today. *Raises eyebrows looking at you* You see it. You know you see it.

I was busy! I was also the oldest child with many responsibilities for my younger brother Ray who was *always* getting into something! The horror of it all! I clearly remember moments as a child where I was pretty much over everything. I did not want to practice, arrange songs, or schedule rehearsals. I did not want to teach Sunday school. I most certainly did not want to be known as the preacher's kid. I could not care less if my shoulders were hunched over or if you could hear me as I walked into a room because my steps were too loud (I'm grateful for charm school now, mom. Really, I am). If good brother Ray didn't eat, so be it. I did not want to do anything but be *"normal."* In my mind, normal kids didn't have to do all of the things that I had to do. Where is the normal kids section? I want to go there.

I journeyed through my teenage years as the odd one. I was fiercely independent, extremely strong-willed, self-motivated, and mature beyond my years. Everything about me from my style of dress, the way I chose to wear my hair, the music I really liked, my thought process, and how I dealt with things were not typical of youth my age. My mother and I can laugh about it now (whew), but to her, I was the strangest little thing and she, at times, did not know what to do with me. Her experiences in the world caused her to desire for me to just go along happily with Jesus, do what I was supposed to do and live as peaceful as possible without causing too many waves. I, on the other hand, was a wave creator. If the other children at the beach stood on the shore line skipping rocks along the water, I was the one with the boulder on a crane (that I'm not supposed to be able to drive by the way), waiting for the right time to drop it so I can see what a massive splash really looks like. No, I was not rebellious. I was different. I always knew that life was so much bigger than what I saw and what I was told. I never followed anyone's word just because. I gave thought to everything that was said. If you told me the moon was made out of cheese, I'd find a way to get there, cracker in hand, to taste it.

SWNM Niya: *Oh, the moon and cheese. Is it pepper jack?*

The transitions young people go through during these years are major! So major that I remember them like it was yesterday. Your body is changing rapidly and you have no control over it. Your emotions are all over the place. It can appear that everything about your parents, church and other adults restricts you. You feel like no one understands you - well, no one but that cute street savvy young man that wants what I now call "your goodness and mercy", or as the elders of the village would call them "those fast tail girls" that have experienced way too much before they were ready.

The pressure during high school and college to decide your whole life (career path, residence, the possibility of marriage and children, etc.) can leave you in a thick fog. You're sprinting towards adulthood with all of this freedom (the equivalent to a drug induced high if not prescribed at the right time and administered correctly) that you're not quite ready for, believing that you are. I know that I did. So, with the wisdom that I acquired through trial and error and the abundant grace of God, I somehow managed, even in the most difficult of situations, to keep it moving, making the best of it. (Again, whatever that means).

At 24 I was a young, educated, vibrant, non-church attending, single woman with a postgraduate degree and nothing to do but work, sleep, and spend my time (and money) however I wanted. I journeyed with no thought for tomorrow, literally. I felt like I had finally reached a place where I did not have responsibilities for anything or anyone but myself. I welcomed this place. I deserved this place. Goodbye safe, dependable one. So long to the one with the answers; the one everyone would solicit to make things right and keep things together. Faithful one, your services are no longer needed. Now it can be about me, myself and I- and I loved it; however, this selfish person that I was trying to be was not who I was created to be. The façade was taking a *major* toll on me that very few recognized. I was enjoyably reckless and unstoppable; that is, until life stopped me. And oh, it stopped me.

My dad called me really late one night to talk. I made it to his home in record time. I could tell from the sound in his voice that something was wrong. When I arrived, he was where he would always be, sitting on the front steps, waiting for me. When I sat down next to him, my dad immediately put his arm around me, then proceeded to tell me that he had cancer. Cancer? Not my dad! Surely the doctor is mistaken. Cancer? I placed my head on my father's shoulders at a total loss of words and began crying uncontrollably. We sat there for hours, saying nothing; but it was one of the best conversations that we had ever had.

In the next few weeks I saw my daddy - this big, strong, tall man full of life - go from my rock who was singing and cracking jokes while being admitted to the hospital to start treatment, to an unresponsive shell. The time between my finding out he had cancer and his departure was a total of three weeks. My father's unexpected death caused me to question everything that I had been taught as a child. His death really became my breaking point. Yes, I believed in God. Yes, I believed in the legitimacy of both Heaven and the Lake of Fire. Yes, I believed that I was to be a good person, love my neighbors, help others, and all the other wonderful Christ-like attributes that I learned and taught in Sunday school, but when "God took my dad," an already functionally reckless me became an extremely angry me, especially at God, and I began to self-destruct. I emotionally shut down and could not care less about most things - church being at the top of that list.

I surprisingly woke up one Sunday morning feeling the need to attend service. After much deliberation, I decided to visit the place where my father's homegoing services were held. I sat there filled with so many conflicting emotions. I was physically present but mentally detached. My mind raced, desperately seeking answers from God as to why He allowed all of these things to happen at this point in my journey. Didn't He know that I needed my dad now more than ever? Didn't he know that I had spent the last 7 years in and out of school and had not been home to see my parents as often as I liked? Why would He do this now?

The more I questioned, the angrier I became. "If God really loves me; if He really knows me like they say He does, He would have at least given me a warning." The angrier I became, the more reckless my thoughts became. "This is foolishness! Why am I here? I've wasted most of my life believing in and praising someone who really cares very little about me. And since He doesn't care, why should I?" I sat there in the service fighting, seeing glimpses of my father's casket as I attempted to look in the front of the church long enough to listen to the pastor. I sat there, internally arguing with myself, convincing myself into staying every time I felt the urge to leave. I sat there, once again making the best of it.

I was asked to help sing a song during the altar call. I declined, however, the pastor would not take "no" for an answer. At some point while singing (I cannot tell you when but at some point), God removed anger and bitterness long enough for me to feel comforted, and for some portion of common sense to kick in. I remember going home after that service feeling more confused than ever. Did I actually enjoy church? Did I actually feel "something" when I sang about God? Wait...I'm still mad at Him.

A memory of a conversation that I had with God in my apartment right before my post-graduate ceremonies replayed over and over again in my mind. Packing up to return home, feeling like a complete lost soul, full of anxiety, regret and a host of other things, I literally fell to my knees in the middle of my living room and cried aloud "God, if I ever step foot in a church again, it's going to be because **You** are teaching and showing me who You are to **me**. I will not serve you based off of what my mom or the church told me is right or wrong. I will not serve You based on who I was told that You are. If I ever go back, it's going to be me and You. Period."

Hindsight is twenty-twenty. Looking back now, I can see life, my incomprehensible journey, striking once again. The death of my father served as the stop that placed me back into church after years of not attending. I was there, struggling, but there nonetheless. Struggling but visiting church more regularly. Struggling but now a member. I started participating in ministry; not fully committed, but actively trying to see if there really was something to this church thing. Yes, something to this church thing. I'm being honest as to where I was at that moment in my life. Have you ever been there? The place where you question the validity of everything you thought you knew because of everything you are currently enduring? You have? Oh, ok.

A last-minute decision to accompany the church on a Sunday school picnic positioned me for a stop along my journey that would change my life forever. At the very end of the night (no really, standing in the funnel cake line, purchasing a snack for the ride home, on my way to the car to leave, "let the church say amen" very end of the night), I connected with a man and a relationship developed. With all of me, I believed that I had been blessed with love, and the rest is my business.

SWNM Niya: *Uhm,* **OUR** *business.*

SWNM MarQuita: *Yup. I guess you're right. Ours. That's it. That's all I have to say about that. I think we're running out of water for the tea anyway. Refill?*

At 25 years of age, I became pregnant. Unmarried and pregnant. I will not spend too much time speaking on this particular topic because I do not want it to overshadow the purpose of this book. Yet I feel the need to share some of my thoughts and experiences regarding it. The repercussions of premarital sex led to my having to live through shame, guilt, gossip, snickers and stares.

SWNM Niya: *I can fight them for you if you want.*

SWNM MarQuita: *You are so your mother's daughter. Put away the sword Peter. I'm ok.*

I lost relationships with people that I thought were my friends because of it. I lost respect for people that I looked up to because of how they handled me at this most fragile point in my life.

Let's start with this: I, in no way, am attempting to justify or glorify premarital sex (or any sin for that matter). I am not dismissing the weight or the wages of any sin. It's death. **Romans 6:23, I Thessalonians 4:3-4, I Corinthians 6:18-19, Galatians 5:19-21, Colossians 3:5**, and many other scriptures admonishes (advises or urges) us to flee (run away from) avoid, abstain (decline, restrain yourself from) fornication. Fornication is sexual intercourse between people who are unmarried. When we disobey the instructions of the Father, we have to be ready to pay the cost. The cost associated with premarital sex is not limited to the possibility of pregnancy, but can include sexually transmitted diseases (some of which are deadly), soul-ties, unnecessary emotional and mental stress, and a tarnished reputation (especially for women). Fornication is sin. All sin is judged. Judgement comes in many forms one of which is correction. Let's talk about correction for a moment. I have an idea. Let's take a poll! Raise your hand if you like correction? Punishment? Keep them high so I can get a good count! No one? No? Interesting.

I truly believe that correction/tough love/rebuke/punishment (whatever you'd like to refer to it as) *without* clear, realistic and attainable goals and boundaries that will lay out how the correction process will directly help the individual (avoiding the default/ one size fit all correction plans) are incorrect. If a person cannot see how the correction will elevate them to a higher place spiritually, or if the correction does not become a point of complete restoration and healing, it becomes useless. If correction is not coupled with healthy Biblical counseling, professional therapy, or other forms of assistance and support, it cannot be sustained. If a person has not or cannot gain a clear understanding of how their actions separated them from the Lord because of the wisdom that should come with correction, the correction can be pointless. I also believe that in those moments where it is decided that open rebuke is necessary it must be handled with care through Godly instruction. We are to always remember that the people of God belong to God. Because of this truth, we are to always rightly divide His Word when it comes to dealing with correction *regardless* of the sin.

Places my tea cup down to readjust myself in my chair. Picks it back up

I'll tell you something else. I have searched scripture high and low and have yet to find the verse that supplies the hierarchy of sin. Is sowing seeds of discord okay? It must be on the low end of the spectrum because it seems to come with only a verbal warning- although it can completely destroy a ministry from the top down. Is deceit and manipulation acceptable? I guess so, although to me it seems to be right along the lines of the deception that Satan used in the Garden of Eden when he beguiled (tricked, charmed, enchanted) Eve. The whole "God didn't say you would surely die" thing is extremely prevalent as we remix scripture to fit our own personal agendas.

What about adultery or womanizing? Are they permissible? Are the wages for a lying tongue compensatory of two Sundays off of the praise and worship team? Are evil thoughts safe from correction? Murder. Is murder unforgivable? I know to some murder has to be way at the other end of the spectrum but is it unforgivable? Somebody please lead me to the scripture (in English please) that states that God will not forgive a repentant soul at the moment they repent.

I'll wait… **Asks question** *One lump or two?*

Leaders and parents, we should never rebuke others based on how we believe their sin will affect our reputations. Correction plans constructed by the ego becomes control. That control can turn into a form of bondage. We also cannot rebuke in order to cause someone embarrassment. A repentant heart is already embarrassed. Trust me! I know leaders who have gone through restoration processes with people and the congregation at large was none the wiser. What's more, the process produced a Kingdom builder.

No, correction does not feel good, but it absolutely has its place. A person who refuses to change their inappropriate behaviors after receiving the aforementioned care (plan of correction) may need an opportunity to think. They may need an assisted pause. They may need to be removed from responsibilities until they can own their part in their deliverance. This takes maturity. Maturity is not solely based on the amount of years that a person has been saved or living. It is based on the condition of their soul.

As the leader of my home I have had to (and will have to continue to because she is human) correct my child. I have had to place my child on punishment (it hurts me to do so) but trust me, she has always known why. She wasn't in the dark as to why she was being corrected, how her actions (when applicable) affected those around her, what we should both expect the correction to bring (the purpose and the end result), that I was correcting her because I love her and that I am an active participant in her process of restoration. Why? I'm learning as well! Ultimately, *we* need to grow. *We* need to be stronger by the end of the process.

SWNM Niya: Well I'm learning that once punishment starts it NEVER stops!

SWNM MarQuita: How about you don't do the things to cause me to have to punish you? *Thinks* That was such a combative parent/leader response, wasn't it? I'll do better next time.

I use to think my mother was insane because she would literally make my brother and I process our correction from beginning to end with her before it started. Who does that? Crazy, right? As an adult, I appreciate it. Her process set the tone for how I deal with correction when it come to my daughter and with others. It also speaks to how I desire to be treated which is with open dialogue, love and again, a clear intentional plan.

If we were to compare the stories of the prodigal son and the woman caught in adultery in an effort to identify "where they went wrong" we *could* argue that both characters within their stories made decisions that were not in their best interest. These decisions led them to live what some may consider "reckless" lives. However, if we continue reading their stories we *could argue* that both characters had intimate encounters with the "father" where they were met with wisdom, instruction, meekness, compassion and with the spirit of restoration.

The father of the prodigal son saw him afar off and was moved to not scold or embarrass him, but to celebrate his return. He didn't even acknowledge when his son said, "I no longer am worthy to be called your son, let me be a servant." The father ignored him and told his servants to bring his son the best he had and to do it now (not in 9 months). Jesus got down in the dirt and removed the power of the accusations from the other human beings (the religious people) surrounding this woman before He said anything to her. There are two major points I want to highlight here:

1. Both individuals had an encounter with the Father that changed their lives. The fathers in each story offered themselves. We do not know how many times either character did what they did. We do not know how many pep talks they may have received prior to their offenses. All we know is that they were offered love when they needed it the most. Question: Can we offer *Jesus* to people?
2. As it was in the Bible, so it is today. Jesus had to remove the naysayers (negative, skeptical, generally gloomy people) first. ⋆*Sigh.*⋆

Some people will never experience the redemptive and restorative love of Christ because of the people surrounding them. Sometimes the people that should be there to help you are the main ones wanting to stone you to death. They really don't want you to come out of what's holding you captive because they know that if you ever become enlightened, if you ever open your mouth to testify or to edify, decree and declare, if you ever walk in the liberty where Christ has set you free they will lose what they consider to be their power, their status, and their security.

Have you ever wondered why we aren't seeing miracles like those we read about in the Bible? Could it be because of our disbelief? Do we want the sick in our churches to remain sick so we can be the healed ones? Do we want the depressed in our churches to remain depressed so we can be the ones in our right minds? Do we really believe that Jesus SAVES? Do we want the lame in our churches to remain lame so we can be the ones with the fanciest foot work? Do we really offer the freedom of Christ to the fallen in its true form? The free indeed form? Jesus waited until the accusers fell off one by one (because none of them were ever without sin) and then he dealt with the woman's sin. He told her, go, and sin no more. I see restoration all up and through these examples. Can we use them?

Yes! He (God) chastens (corrects) whom He loves. Yes! But thank God that when He comes into a situation He comes to give life, and life more abundantly. He did not come to condemn the world but He came that the world through Him might be saved **(John 3:17)**.

Religious practice saves no one. Revelation of the cross does. How many souls have left the body of Christ because we do not operate in our ability and mandate to restore those that have fallen with the spirit of meekness? No, restoration does not remove consequences, but it sure gives hope. Isn't it hope that does not put us to shame? **Romans 5:3-5** reads, "Not only that, but we rejoice in our sufferings, knowing that suffering produces endurance, endurance produces character, and character produces hope, and hope does not put us to shame, because God's love has been poured into our hearts through the Holy Spirit who has been given to us." Well, when did this happen **verse 6**? "For while we were still weak, at the **RIGHT TIME** Christ died for the ungodly." Hold the phone!

*SWNM Niya: *Picks up her actual cell phone and declares* "Hello, I'm holding the phone!" **LOL!***

*SWNM MarQuita: *Laughs hysterically* I cannot with you Niya.*

Love met these characters not after they were cleaned up, brushed off, sanctified and set apart. Love met them at their mess. Their mess was the right time! *Hands flew up in praise. Tears are filling my eyes* Thank you Jesus for your mercy!

Beloved, we have hope only because of God's love. Speaking of love, it starts at home (Luke 4:23) and then it spreads itself abroad. We can foster all of these wonderful outreach and evangelism efforts, but they will fail to reap a harvest until we can get down with those buried in the dirt in our own backyards, helping them to pull the weeds that are preventing them from having a fruitful walk with Christ and then nurse them back to health. Christ as our Redeemer and our Lord is the One who can completely blot out our sins and give us a fresh new start. I humbly repented and asked God for His forgiveness for my disobedience almost 16 years ago, and He did just that. I am so grateful. The sweetest tea of all is that since He's done it for me, I know He can do it for you!

It was an ongoing process, but through much prayer and support from the safe people that God gave me, I started to let my guard down and open my heart again. To what? To my journey. During this time in my life, I began to release the anger I felt towards God. Knowing that I was carrying another life changed my perspective. First, I recognized that only God could give life. The fact that He gave me the ability to carry life instead of immediately taking mine, that He protected me and did not allow me to contract a deadly disease or something worse was enough to bring me to a place of complete gratitude and humility. Secondly, I did not want my child bathing in a womb full of negativity juices so I knew that I had to change my thoughts, my actions, and my priorities from the inside out. God had given this soul a gift, and that gift became the gift that saved my life.

SWNM Niya: Yessir!

I found myself praying more. I anointed my belly faithfully and cried out saying, "God, you gave her to me. I give her back to you. Her spirit was given a soul at this time for a purpose. I am her mother on purpose. I have to be whole so she can be whole. I have to heal so I can teach her how to heal. I have to stand tall so she will never have a reason to hang her head in shame. I have to live for you so she will."

I became very strategic with everything I spoke to her, about her, over her, and her journey into this world. My daughter's very name means purpose, intended, and champion. I rejected anything or anyone who tried to diminish the blessing of who she was to be, not only to me but to the world. Sharing our story excites me! Why? **WE SURVIVED!** We're alive! We overcame! Neither of us are angry or bitter. We're better; so much better!

SWNM Niya: #BetterNotBitter

Niya is **Romans 8:28** in action in my life! She is all things (yes, all) working together for my good. Even in what appeared to be the craziest of places, God knew that in my heart I loved Him, and that I was called according to His purpose. I had a journey with a mission to fulfill and so did she.

Niya is **Isaiah 61:3**! She is beauty for ashes, she brought joy when I should have been mourning, her life gave me praise in thanksgiving for grace, mercy, and forgiveness and I chose not to die in heaviness. Our lives are a testimony because through it all, we stood strong and united together like trees that God planted and HE, in all things, has been glorified. As I traveled around singing, it has been my daughter working my product tables. As I'm aspiring to share the gospel of Jesus Christ through the preached Word, it has been my daughter holding me up, praying for me, and covering me. As I work the altar, it has been my daughter down on the floor pleading the "blood of Jesus" with me. When I want to give up and revert back to the me of the past, I look at her and see all of the reasons why I must continuously strive to become a better person than I've ever been. Niya is scripture fulfilled. God took a decision that I made that the enemy could have used to kill everything about me and made it beautiful. She came at the appointed time. She came at the right stop in my journey.

SWNM Niya: I'm touched. Thanks, sweetheart.

SWNM MarQuita: Well it's true. I cannot imagine my life without you.

Niya

I really do not know what to say. Learning about how I came into this world and how much my mother endured for me is crazy. She told me the story before, but it's different when it's right in front of you. My mom went through a lot during her pregnancy, but it was all worth it because I'm here :) right Mom? LOL!

She was so strong. She is probably the strongest person I know. She found her way back to God when she really didn't want to and she was able to give me back to God. People looked at her sideways for having a baby out of wedlock but that never stopped her from providing and loving me. She is the best-est most awesome-est mom ever and I'm glad God gave her to me. Thank you for all that you did and thank you for all that you're doing! I love you!

MarQuita: Awe! ★ ***With tear filled eyes*** *I love you too Moo!* ***Blows kisses and reaches for her neck***

Niya: Mom!!!!! ***Smacks arm away***

MarQuita: What?? I do love you. Come here!! ***Reaches out again with the pouty lips***

Niya: ***Walks away rolling eyes***

This is how we do it:

A lot was shared between the introduction and this chapter. Let's dive right into further discussion.

- **(M)** Relationship outweighs religious practice. Jesus purposely spent time in His earthy ministry showing us that there was a better way to God; one that religious pomp and circumstance or practice (practice: the act of carrying out of performing a particular activity, method, or custom habitually or regularly) could never provide. That way is relationship via grace, for by grace we are saved through faith. **(Ephesians 2:8)** Religion brings the letter of the law, but grace allows us to operate in relationship. Grace is a gift! The gift that keeps on giving!

  Do you know that the great big God of the universe desires to commune with us completely? He rejoices when we come to Him in moments of happiness or in despair. He is a consistent God, so His love for us will never change whether He is comforting or correcting. Understanding God's unconditional love (it really takes faith to comprehend it) frees us to enter into relationship. We are always safe there. God won't tell our secrets, He won't make fun of our folly, and He won't turn his back on us.

- **(M)** Forgive yourself and forgive others. It may seem like it is the hardest thing to do, (and to be truthful, sometimes it is), but forgiving yourself and forgiving others is the *best* thing (outside of serving Jesus) that you could ever do. When you lack forgiveness for others, you interfere with the Father's ability to forgive you. A lack of forgiveness makes us rotten to our very core, which is the place where love is to reside for God is love.

  We must pray for the ability to "let some folk off the hook." (I know...I know...Breathe! Slow steady breaths) Yes, they hurt you. Yes, they have done you wrong (knowingly or maybe unknowingly.) Consider yourself. Understand that forgiveness is not contingent upon whether you receive an apology or not. God is not holding you accountable for other people's actions. He is holding you accountable for your journey.

Here's another way to think about it: Forgiveness gives you an opportunity to give to others what they may not be able to give to you. Most of the times they cannot offer you forgiveness because they cannot offer it to themselves. Another point to consider is that forgiving others does not bound you to remaining in fellowship with them. There are examples within the Bible of people who had differences in opinions and decided to go their separate ways. (Read **Acts 15:30-41**) You have nothing to prove.

From the middle of 2015 to the present, I have literally received multiple text messages, inboxes, and phone calls from individuals apologizing to me for things that they have done to me. Some of these apologies are for things that were done years ago. I could have (if pettiness resided within me) taken these individuals through a series of questions, guilt trips, and released the wrath of my anger but why would I do that? Who is that helping? Is that Christ like? Or better yet, would a disciple of Jesus respond that way? Would I want that to be done to me? No. I have not asked one of these individuals for an explanation. Through the grace of God, I was able to reply, "All is forgiven."

You also are forgiven. When you are caught in a fault, sincerely repent to God (repentance means to forsake and turn completely away from), seek out the path to the truth, gain insight as to why this was or is an area of weakness for you, honor the wisdom and guidance of your accountability partner, and be honest with yourself and others.

Pray and seek the Lord, then as Jesus told the woman caught in adultery in **John 8**, "Go, and sin no more." You cannot afford to throw your entire life's journey away based on one moment in time. Forgive yourself so you can be free from the guilt. Guilt is cancerous. It will eat you up from the inside out. Christ paid the price at Calvary for any and everything you will ever do. Oh, yes He did! We dare not disrespect His death on the cross by living any ole kind of way (help us Jesus), but He took all the shame so you and I would not have to! Look at yourself in the mirror and repeat after me: "I was worth His life. He died so that I can live. I will live. I will live free of guilt and forgive myself from this moment forward."

I had to forgive myself for introducing my child to something that I vowed that I would never do, which is birth her into an unwed household. Growing up, I wanted nothing more than to know what it felt like to be raised in a two-parent home. My parents were indeed married, so I was born into a home with both, but have very few memories of it. I use to beat myself up unmercifully day in and day out thinking about the conversations I would have to have with her because I was not married when she was conceived. I tried to brace myself for the disappointment I believed that I would see in her eyes when she left the homes of her friends (who had both parents) to come back to a home with just me. The mental abuse I put myself through was unbearable; until the light bulb went off and I realized a few things:

- Children are more resilient than we give them credit. Yes, there were times where my daughter had "the look" and I had to console her, sharing my upbringing while reassuring her that I knew what she was feeling and that she was going to be ok. However, at no time was she deep in despair, rolling around sulking, nor did she (surprising to me) feel that she was lacking anything.

- Unfortunately, there are some children born in wedlock, living in two parent homes that are flat out miserable. They witness their parents fight all of the time. They witness division on a daily basis. If these things are not present, their parents fail to invest in their futures, fail at talking to them (outside of giving directives in discipline), nor do they spend time with them.

I am ever so grateful for any household that does not display the aforementioned qualities as this is not a good environment for any child whether the parents are married or not.

I honor marriage. I honor those families where the children were born in wedlock. I was not going to marry or guilt trip a man into wanting to marry me because I was pregnant. I was not going to subject my child to live through the pain we cause when we force things together to keep people from talking about us. They're going to talk anyway. They're talking now while reading this book trying to find a reason to be offended, or justify ignorance, or prove me wrong. Bless you. Who has time for that?

My mission is to reach those that have experienced what I have to show them that God still has need of them. Niya has been blessed tremendously. She is abundantly loved. People have always gravitated towards her. There's a light within her that is undeniable. She has been covered with grace. This is her testimony. What is not a part of her testimony (and I pray that it never will be) is divorced parents. Amen.

- **(M)** Acceptance. Acceptance for me is simple. It is relinquishing my right to fight. MarQuita is synonymous with fighter. By nature, I can go into "fight mode" without thinking. (I am daily lifting this up to the Lord for His divine assistance for when and when not to fight. If He does not hear me, I know He hears my dear mother who keeps this front and center in her prayers also. LOL!)

Here's the thing about fighters. Fighters do not play patty cake with an opponent, unless they are bored. Fighters seek to annihilate and eliminate whatever is standing in their way. I've grown to understand that in life, especially in my spiritual journey, there are things that I cannot fight with my natural hands. **Ephesians 6:12** teaches me that I am not wrestling against flesh and blood, but rather, this fight is against principalities, powers, the rulers of darkness of this world, and spiritual wickedness in high places.

In other words, I'm fighting things I cannot see, things I cannot touch, things that live in a realm where I do not, but also dwell in the earth where I am. For these things, I can fight, but on my knees in prayer and by way of fasting and consecration. For the weapons of my warfare are not carnal, but mighty, not through me, but through God for the intentions (see, this fight has purpose) of pulling down strongholds, casting down imaginations, and every high thing that exalteth itself against the knowledge of God, and bringing into captivity every thought to the obedience of Christ **(II Corinthians 10:4-5)**.

With all of my wit and intelligence, strength and power, and ability to normally make things happen, I am not in control over everything. (You owe God a praise for that even now!) God is in control, especially over this thing called life. I find refuge in His Word in times of need. I learn that the battle belongs to God in **II Chronicles 20:15**. I learn that I need to just hold my peace in **Exodus 14:14**. I learn that although I see an enemy today, it'll be the last day in **Exodus 14:13**, and I learn that vengeance belongs to God in **Romans 12:19**. I'm taught to be anxious for nothing in **Philippians 4:6-7**. He tells me He knows how to give good gifts in **Luke 12:29,** and that if He takes care of the lilies of the field, He'll take care of me in **Luke 12:27**. He reigns over the just as well as the unjust and time, time is truly in His hands. My job is to let God be God, and rest in that.

• **(M)** Honor Leadership. As previously stated, no leader (in any capacity) is God. However, once you make a decision to join/accept your position, be it at a company, an institute of higher education, in a marriage, or in a church ministry, you agree to abide within the context of that relationship. Most people do not take the time to thoroughly educate themselves regarding the rules, regulations, or expectations, nor do they read the fine print of memberships. Membership has its privileges but it also has it stipulations. If you conduct a survey and ask faithful church members why they are members of their respective churches, you would receive answers that span anywhere from the skill of the church band to the excitement of the Bible class. Truth is that we should all be at our churches for no other reason than God placing us there. Some are born into certain churches. I understand. Here's a question for you: Has God told you to remain where you were born? Have you ever thought to ask Him? I'm just asking.

When contemplating church membership, it may be helpful to have a pre-membership class or counseling session with leadership. This class or session, much like premarital counseling, should be a place where you can ask all of those real hard questions before you decide to join. For example: A question that I would ask leadership if I was contemplating membership would be, "How do you handle open rebuke?" (Are you shocked? Why would I ask that? LOL) I've lived through it several times and it was not the highlight of my 41 years. If the leaders' response is anywhere near my experience or if they verbalize that they make anyone at any time sit on the front bench in complete silence every Sunday after confessing their private sin in front of everyone, I know God is not sending me there. There's no need for me to pass go or collect two hundred dollars. How do I know? I do not agree with that course of discipline. I would not be able to respect the leader. It is very difficult to honor what you do not respect.

Understand that in their humanity, leaders will make mistakes also. Prayerfully each leader has a leader that they are accountable to, someone that can give them good counsel and instructions, and pray with them when they sin. A leader who can admit their mistakes and grow in grace by learning how to handle situations better as they serve God's people deserves double honor. Leaders who refuse to learn and are so calloused that souls are being negatively affected are dangerous. You may see it, you may want to stop it, and you may want to say something about it, but beware! Just because the authority is abused, does not mean the authority is not legitimate. I was taught not to speak against pastors, but rather step back, and let God handle them. (Remember, God will fight your battle.) Honoring leadership comes with a serious benefits package.

Think of all of the patrons in the Bible as well as those you know present day that are blessed because they serve those serving God, accepted correction, and maintained faith in the process of becoming better. Follow your leader as they follow Christ **(I Corinthians 11:1)**. No, correction does not feel good at the moment. It's painful and unpleasant, but it yields peaceable fruit of righteousness to those who have been trained by it **(Hebrew 12:11).** The fruit yielded from that judgment comes to save us from being condemned with the world **(I Corinthians 11:32).**

I've been blessed to have wonderful pastors at different points in my journey. All of them human (LOL). I have not agreed with everything that they have said or done. Even so, my place was to honor them. Each of them have taught me valuable lessons that will stay with me for my lifetime. Memories with them causes my heart to smile and, in most cases, laugh. Correction from them have caused me to grow.

• **(N)** You can have your tea hot or cold but the truth ain't debatable. Embrace the truth. That is all that I have to say.

Prayer

Father I thank you for you are good and your mercy endures forever. I praise you for being the only true and living God. You have revealed yourself to me and to my daughter in ways that are unimaginable; for this I give you praise. I ask that you bless everyone reading this book. I ask that you allow us to understand that your grace is sufficient, your mercy is plentiful, and your love covers every stop along our life journey. I ask you to remove the sting from those of us that are dealing with guilt from our past. Let us now, at this very moment, allow you to come in to heal us and to break the shackles of bondage that the enemy has attempted to place over our hearts, minds, mouths, spirits, body and souls. We declare that He whom the son has set free is free indeed. Give us the power to forgive ourselves and others. Reveal your plan of restoration to leadership and to churches in the Kingdom worldwide. Don't allow us to kill what you have given purpose. Help us to consistently operate in agape love. Speak words of life into every dead place. We shall live and not die. We shall declare your good works in the land of the living. Help us to accept those things that we do not understand, and grant us the knowledge to know how to properly manage those things that are in our control. Fight our battles God. Provide us with wisdom as we make decisions to stand still or move, to keep silent or to speak. Let us not be foolish, but reverent, acknowledging your sovereignty as Lord of all. Give everyone a hunger and thirst after righteousness, for you promised in your Word that if we hunger and thirst after it, we shall be full. We need right relationship with you God. Restore our families. Help us to allow the power of the gift of your Holy Spirit to keep us from falling. Give us one mind, and let it be yours. We thank you in advance.

In the name of Jesus we pray, Amen.

3

Tackling Transition

Lynn

Change. It's that thing that moves your favorite song from the verse to the hook. It's the decision that develops, ignites and then catapults you from a place of stagnation to a place of triumph. Change is inevitable. It will either happen all at once or it will happen in such a way that it will cause evolution over time. You cannot effectively transition without changing. Let me provide an example that some of you ladies can probably relate to.

I wake up one day and I decide that I want my permed hair back in its natural, chemical-free state again. I can change it immediately by cutting it all off and starting fresh (the big chop which is more of a physical act) or I can choose to transition- cutting the perm off from the ends of the hair little by little until it is completely gone (which is more mental and emotional). By transitioning, I am taking my time. While allowing the new growth to come in healthy, I also maintain as much length as possible for as long as possible. This should help by decreasing my level of anxiety and everything else you can imagine would come along with a change such as this one.

I truly believe that in order to successfully transition throughout our life's journey, we have to be able to accept the need for change and be able to acknowledge that change will occur, whether we want it to or not. Once this is accomplished, we must prepare. For transition is a verb, an action word, therefore it requires such.

Is it just me or does anyone else find that transition has a way of appearing when you least expect it in the areas of your life where you are fully content? Between 2013 and 2016, my life seemed to be a revolving door of endless transitions. In June of 2013, in what seemed to be at the height of my career, I was laid off from an employer that I had work with for seven years due to a lack of funding. That's life within the not-for-profit sector; however, it wasn't supposed to be my life. My plan was to retire from this organization. Through the grace of God, I had steadily moved up the ranks and was now at a place that felt good to me. I was the active Administrator over Children's Services, responsible for the foster/kinship care, aftercare, and adoption units as well as the certification of homes and training divisions. I worked with a wonderful group of people (those that I supervised and those that supervised me) and was quite happy about it. We worked hard. We serviced so many families through a variety of programs that really made a difference in the community.

Employment also opened up opportunities to minister. (I mean really, how can you work in child welfare or social services, believe in God, and He not come up in the conversations while you're speaking to clients on a continual basis about "coming up and coming out?" Of course, you must have these conversations very carefully and with wisdom, allowing the client to initiate them. Shh! Don't tell anyone that I told you!) My organization honored me with the highly respected *Staff Award* for providing outstanding leadership, compassion, vision and service, an honor that I was able to share with my daughter and my mother. Niya pretty much grew up there. She was able to attend the daycare on campus, transitioning into the summer camp as she got older. I had just released my first EP entitled *Free* in December of 2012 and was traveling a lot. My employer supported my efforts. Everything was well and my soul was at peace. So, God, about this layoff thing...

As the head of my household, I instantly became concerned about the things that most responsible caregivers would – for example, the mortgage payment, the car note, the electricity, gas, and the water. Our hair still needed to be done, we had to eat, and still needed to get away on vacation. I was determined that my daughter would not experience any lack. How to make my determination a reality was something different. I collected unemployment from June 2013 through December 2013. In January 2014, the government bill that was needed in order for myself and thousands (maybe millions) of other people to continue receiving the unemployment compensation that we've worked for was not passed. Our ability to collect ended abruptly and was not reinstated.

2014 was my year of *extreme* faith. I found myself desperately looking for jobs and nothing was coming through, mainly because I was overqualified (or at least that's what I was told.) I grieved the loss of employment. Although I did my best to maintain the lifestyle my daughter was accustomed to, I had to make drastic changes if we were going to survive. My brother Ray and sister-in-love Lauren were such a blessing to my household, as was my faithful mother and my auntie/mom Mary Alice. Aunt Alice has always been there supporting everything that I have ever done in every way imaginable. She has been an angel on earth. God showed me how to use what I saved (yes, saved; we'll touch on finances in another chapter), and the income that I received while ministering on the road to keep our house afloat. Our utilities were never turned off. Our home was not foreclosed. I actually paid off our car. Niya went on more major trips and vacations in that single year than she had ever gone (and she was always on the go!)

I cannot say that I did not have moments where the pressure did not get to me. I did. Oh, but just when it felt like the pressure was going to grind me to shreds, God would send someone my way and they would place money in my hand. Someone would call and give me the words that I needed to live by. I did not have to ask for one thing because my Father truly supplied all of my needs - my mental needs, my spiritual needs, my emotional needs and yes, my financial needs. He did it through unexpected channels and through unexpected people. By the end of 2014, I was gainfully employed. I still thank God for this job every time I walk through the door.

The greatest gift I received during this transition was increased faith. No lie. My faith muscles are solid as a rock! As time and chance happens to those around me, I've had to flex those muscles unashamed to share my story and encourage others who were going through the same thing I went through years ago. I am able to tell them, without wavering, that God can do the impossible. He specializes in those types of things. Isn't it amazing?

SWNM Niya: It is amazing :).

After years of praying and conversations with leadership, I decided that January 2015 was the time to change my membership from the assembly that I attended for the past 15 years (14 and some change to be exact.) If you've ever transitioned from a church, you know all that it entails. If you haven't, let me share that it is not easy, especially when you were fully invested in the ministry, fully invested in the people of the ministry, and worked hard while there. I was heavily concerned with the following:

- How do I tell the pastor that I believe my *season* (you all know we love the word *season* over here in holiness) has come to an end?

Check! My former pastor and I had been speaking on this for a long time. Although the set time was unknown, the need to transition was made clear and God allowed me to thoughtfully, respectfully, intelligently, and spiritually communicate it. I was leaving in good standing. My mother told me from childhood never to leave a place wrong because you always want to be able to return should the need arise. I'm glad that I listened to her.

- How do I answer all of the questions about my departure and deal with the gossip that was sure to come?

Check! I had already come to peace with the knowledge that people are going to talk regardless, especially when you are not giving them any information as to why you are doing what you are doing. Those I shared my decision with initially were those I trusted to pray for my family. I chose to keep silent about my next steps. I dealt with it by living, and paying no attention to the talk. When you have the truth surrounding you, you have no room for fear, for the truth fills all spaces.

- How do I tell Niya and how do I help her to navigate through this major change?

This is the only church she has ever known. Her friends are here. People we consider family are here. This place was a constant in her life's journey. I knew from the beginning that I would have to have several conversations with Niya. I tried to be very surface with her in the beginning, but that did not last for long. (Of course it wouldn't. She's my child.) As I explained why I felt the need to transition, Niya began to understand. That's what I needed; her understanding not her agreement. I shared the story of Abraham with her. Abraham left on the word of the Lord from the familiar, from his family, not knowing the exact place that he and his family were going, but he went trusting that God would not let him fail. I told her, "Niya, God will not let us fail" and He has not. He has actually showed us, as He has always shown us, that if we trust in Him with all of our heart, not leaning to our own understanding, acknowledging Him in all of our ways, that He would truly direct our paths. **(Proverbs 3:5-6)**

It took some time (two years' worth of sleeping/resting, visiting, praying, fasting, spitting, snotting, questioning and questioning again), but we are now members of a wonderful church that we call home. To be honest, I fought the voice of the Lord for a long time regarding our membership here. I had already respected the pastor from afar for many years. He was a preacher and teacher par excellence. His ability to break down the Word of God reminded me so much of the Bishop of my childhood. He is musically inclined, very well respected, still youthful, and STATES AWAY? No sir, King Jesus! You mean to tell me that you do not have a church home in this great big city for my family? We must drive to another state to go to church? Have you seen the gas prices? Do you know how much wear and tear that's going to put on my car? Do you know how much time we'll spend on the road alone? No. I refused to believe it was true, yet I knew that He was calling us there.

I remember sitting up in the bed one Sunday while Niya and I watched television. I simply said to God in a private prayer, "Okay Lord. I'm tired. Please reveal to me where we are supposed to be. I promise I won't fight you anymore." Instantly, God told me the name of my pastor. I saw his face as clear as day. We were there that Sunday. We joined soon after.

I think we can all agree that money and church are major areas of transition. So are relationships and friendships. Those were transitioning too. (We'll talk about these in a later chapter). With so much happening at the same time, you can really find yourself emotionally and mentally drained; a disconnected shell of your former self. This is dangerous; especially when another life is depending on you.

Up to this point, this chapter was pretty much about Me. Me. Me. All about me. Yeah right. It can never be all about me. LOL! While I was transitioning, so was my child. I'm not going to speak too much on this as I want you to read her thoughts. However, as a parent I had to honor that we were both working through our uncomfortable moments at the same time. If I'm emotionally and mentally drained, so is she. If I'm fighting to keep my attitude in check, so is she. If I'm confused about what and who I should believe in, so is she.

We are both learning how to navigate through the moments where you find yourself surrounded by people and those where you are completely alone. We are both living in moments of what appears to be ultimate success and moments which appear to be utter failure. It's all a part of this journey. As her parent, I had to remain as equally invested in her process as I was in mine. This was not always easy to do. There are moments where you do not want to have to think about anyone else. Moments where you want to climb in the bed, throw the covers over your head and come out a week later. Moments when you don't want to be the adult. (I just envisioned throwing myself to the ground kicking and screaming). Yeah. I want to do that, but alas, I cannot and for the sake of my daughter, I will not.

SWNM Niya: Good job mom!

We'll all transition until the Lord sees fit to call us to rest. Allowing yourself to evolve takes guts. People will attempt to place you in their box and dare you to burst out. I've never been one to back down from a challenge. (See, you are not praying. Didn't I tell you all to pray against this fighting spirit?) Our bodies transition. They change without permission. The seasons change without permission. People will change, and they will do it without permission. The only thing that remains constant in an inconsistent world is God. **Ecclesiastes 3:1-8** speaks so eloquently to this point: "For everything there is a season, and a time for every matter under the heaven: A time to be born, and a time to die; a time to plant, and a time to pluck up what is planted; A time to kill, and a time to heal; a time to break down, and a time to build up; A time to weep, and a time to laugh; a time to mourn, and a time to dance; A time to cast away stones, and a time to gather stones together; a time to embrace, and a time to refrain from embracing; A time to seek, and a time to lose; a time to keep, and a time to cast away; A time to tear, and a time to sew; a time to keep silence, and a time to speak; A time to love, and a time to hate; a time of war, and a time of peace."

Remember, time is that invisible yet ever-present partner on your journey. It is filled with transitions. *How* you transition will determine your victories. Don't be afraid to tackle them straight on. The Bible is clear; in the end, we win! I'll ride with those odds any day!

Simone

> "Trust in the LORD with all thine heart; and lean not
> unto thine own understanding." **Proverbs 3:5**

Transition is something that everyone will have to experience. To transition means to go from one step to another step in life, no matter how big or small. I've been through alot of transitions and I've learned a lot in the process. Things absolutely happen for a reason. I know it sounds cliché, but it's true.

I was only thirteen when we started to write this book, so I do not remember everything. My mom has always been big on taking a lot of pictures and videos. Because of this, I can see my growth. I went from not being able to move much, to crawling, walking, and then to running. I was told that when I first started to walk and run, people had to walk closely to me protecting my head because I would always run into the church benches. I've grown a lot since then, even though I still have a habit of walking into things today. LOL! I've seen pictures when I didn't have any teeth, to having teeth, to not having teeth again, to having my adult teeth. I remember singing in the kitchen in my plastic princess heels and dancing with the broom. Again, I don't remember everything about my childhood but the things I remember are great.

Looking at my old elementary school report cards, awards, and certificates, I think I was a pretty good student. I was settled, but just when I thought I had it all together, it would be time for me to decide where I wanted to go to school next. I remember it like it was yesterday. Third grade year. My mom and I were driving to go shopping when I saw this building. I asked her to pull over. I looked at the building and then I looked back at my mom and said "Mom, I'm going to go to this school one day." My mom was clueless that it was actually a school, but she got out of the car on my word, wrote the name of the school down and did her mommy research. It was then that we found out that it was a highly respected, special admissions magnet school known for its musical accomplishments. We took the steps to apply.

When the time came for me to audition, I was really nervous. I was only in the fourth grade! The staff hosting the auditions told me to sing the song that I had prepared and gave me a small note recognition test. With the Lord's help, I got through the audition successfully. When my mom got the news that I was accepted she sent flowers to my elementary school. When she came to pick me up I asked her what were the flowers for. My mom told me that I was accepted into the school of my choice! I was so excited.

Once you hit middle school, you think you've grown up. That is, until you see a much older, much bigger, and much smarter kid walking down the hallway. Attending a new school is very nerve racking. I was terrified because I didn't know anyone and I thought I was going to be alone, but I wasn't. I meet many friends that comforted me in my early middle school days. After spending four years at that school, I know I have grown in so many ways. Initially, I was a shy little girl who never wanted to sing in front of anyone, but now I can sing and audition for things with little fear. Attending this school really helped me come out of my shell.

Thankfully, I survived the process of transitioning from middle school to high school. My mom kept telling me that high school would be a different experience. This automatically put more pressure on me to be better in every way because I wanted to be accepted in this new "world". I wanted to be a good student and have good friends like I did in elementary school. My mom reminded me that if you have one good friend, you have the world and that's all you need, but to me one is just not enough. I do have my best friend, but sometimes I still want other friends that I can hang out with in school and outside of school, in church and outside of church.

In time, I eventually gained more friends. I just had to be myself around people which helped me to find the right group. Mom also told me that everything I'm doing now is preparing me for my future. I knew the work was going to get much harder and that I could not let my grades slip because it could impact everything in a negative way. I had to work, knowing that everything I did was contributing to my future. I'm glad to say that the transition was not as hard as it could have been and freshman year wasn't as bad as I thought it would have been. Mom was right. Middle school and high school are different, but school is still school at the end of the day. You have to get the work done to be successful, and that's not only in school but in life too. My freshman year I did a lot. By this, I mean I participated in alot. I was in varsity cheerleading, construction crew for our plays, our school Broadway musical, yearbook committee, hop committee (like prom committee), in concert choir, started playing the trumpet and was in the Philadelphia All City Choir. I was even a manager for the girls' basketball team for a short period of time. Juggling all those things wasn't easy, but it was worth it. I experienced much and I'm glad, because it was a lot of fun. What wasn't easy was doing all those extra activities and trying to keep my grades up. Somehow, I made it through the year without failing every class. If that's not God, then I don't know what is!

Enough about school. I am a teenager. Turning 13 really wasn't as special as I expected it to be. The only thing that came with being 13 that was different from being 12 is being able to say that I'm 13, which means I'm a teenager. Other than that, there's no difference. Then I turned 14 which felt the same as 13. Nothing big happened. I just gained a little more responsibility.

For example, when I was younger, my mom stayed on top of me about my homework all of the time. She'd ask me was it done, was it done well, and then she checked it. Now my mom doesn't bother me as much as she used to, so I have to be responsible and self-motivated to get my work done. She still asks if it was done, but she told me that she is slowly but surely stepping back as I get older because I will have to make sure that I do my own homework when I go to college. Nothing big though.

I've also noticed that I cannot get away with as much as I used to like saying "I didn't know" or leaving little things lying around the house. Nope. My mom notices all of that now. I know. Nice try, right? Again, what can I say? Being 15 wasn't much different. One thing that did happen at 15 was braces! My braces didn't hurt when I first got them, but I couldn't eat a lot. It felt weird at first because there was always something in my mouth, but I quickly got used to it. I can't wait to get them off though! Oh, and let me not forget to mention the wonderful raise in my allowance! 15 brought me more money!

To me, your teenage years are just another period of time that you have to live through. It's special though, because you're developing into your own person. You're going to be able to take on more responsibilities. You'll want to go more places on your own because your mom is embarrassing. (What? Who said that! LOL!)

SWNM MarQuita: I am not! You know you love having me around.

Anyway, you are going to want your parents to trust you so you can do what you want. I'm not saying they'll let you do everything but they'll start to consider it more ***Whispers*** Try not to do anything that will mess up their trust ok?

Parents, teenagers develop more and more with each transition. I think this is one of the most important times of transition in our lives. The thing is, we might not always know the best way to handle it. There are a lot of feelings that come with being a teenager. I've discovered that I am more emotional, more opinionated, and I can be angered more easily. Let me explain! I am more emotional (hint hint), but sometimes I don't know where all of these emotions come from. All I know is that they are there. I try to control them but sometimes I can't. There are times when I feel that my mom is nagging me just to see my reaction.

SWNM MarQuita: Excuse me? Nagging you just to get a reaction? I wish! ***Bows back out***

When I retaliate from her nagging, it looks like I'm being spoiled but to me, her nagging was unreasonable.

SWNM MarQuita: Retaliate? There's retaliation?

It's like that person that won't stop talking during a really good movie. I'm going to want to tell them to leave me alone, but I can't say this to her because she's still my mom. I have to respect her. This, at times, seems unfair because if the tables were turned my mom would be able to tell me to leave her alone. I start to become aggravated and upset. When that starts to become noticeable, we have a problem.

I would like to believe that the feelings I have are wrong because my mom has done so much for me, but I just can't help it. I think everyone can agree that no one likes the person talking in the movie theater. I've always been opinionated, but now that has increased. I notice that if I feel strongly about something, I won't keep it to myself. I will voice my opinion. When I try to stay quiet, my facial expressions tell it all. With all of these feelings mixed with all of these transitions and things not always going as planned, I can be angry. Anger can cloud good judgment. Unfortunately, when you are angry, you can make the wrong decisions for yourself. Since I've realized this, I try my best not to let that happen.

I'm glad to say that even though I've changed, in some ways I've stayed the same. I still like to have fun with my friends and family, get my nails done, be silly, and I still love to create. My mother always tells me not to be in a rush to grow up and I'm not. I'm not one of those kids that wants to be all grown and stuff. Sure, sometimes I might want to wear something a little "grown for my age" but nothing too crazy. My mom wouldn't allow it anyway. The main reason I don't want to grow up is because I don't want adult responsibility. Unfortunately, I know it's coming and there's nothing I can do about it.

In 2015, I transitioned from the church I went to all of my life. For the most part, all of my friends were at that church. Initially I did not know how to adjust so I kept all of my feelings bottled in trying to come to an understanding within myself. I thought leaving was unfair and that I was going to lose my friends. My mom comforted me by saying real friends remain friends no matter the distance. She was right. My true friends have remained my friends. At first, it felt like we were just leaving that church because she didn't like it there. That wasn't it at all. My mom explained her experiences and what she now wanted for the both of us. That helped me cope with things a little better. This is why communication is really important (especially in big transitions). I would have never known the truth if I didn't ask. Talking about it helped everything become better for me. (We'll talk more about communication in a different chapter.) I am now at peace and looking forward to what's next.

Just know, there are many transitions that we all are going to have to go through. Some are going to be tougher than others. As long as you have a person to take the transition with you and God, everything will be alright.

"In all thy ways acknowledge Him, and he shall direct thy paths."
Proverbs 3:6

This is how we do it:

- **(L)** Do not curse God and die. Pressure will have you saying things and reacting in ways that you normally would not. God allowed me to recognize that what I spoke and how I handled transition, especially at this point in my life, would dictate what He could trust me with. There were moments where I thought I was going to lose my very mind and moments that I did not want to live anymore. There were times when the enemy attempted to take me back to the days of questioning what I shared with you in the previous chapters. Times when I would try to make sense of why God would allow me to go through these test and trials if He really loves me.

Stronger now, anointed for this journey now, fixated on the word now in relationship with God I was able to confess to the enemy, "I will not curse God and die." If you have not read the story of Job in the Bible, make it your business to do so. He lost everything; but because he remained faithful, in the end God gave him twice as much as he had before. Greater than his material wealth, the Kingdom gained a victory because Job did exactly what God knew he would: he journeyed on remaining devoted.

- **(L)** Remain faithful to God's instructions while you are in transition. At the end of December 2012, God instructed me to sow $100 a month into a person that He would direct me to for the entire year of 2013. I willingly said yes, and did as He commanded without second thought. When June 2013 came around and I was laid off from my job, I, in a moment of panic, questioned whether I could get a pass on giving to others because I needed to make sure that my household would survive. I kind of alluded to God that I thought His will had changed and that it was alright for me to hold off on giving, which He corrected me immediately on. He kind of had a *SWNM* with me!

SWNM Niya: *Insert thunder and lightning*

There absolutely was no change in His mind on the instructions that He had given me. I got myself together and continued to sow the money and, in turn, reaped an abundant harvest. When God gives you instructions, He doesn't change them just because life took you by surprise. God knew that unemployment was going to meet me at the middle of the year. He actually sent someone to prophesy to me that it was going to occur three days before it happened. My faithfulness sent a message to my transition that I was going to stay the course come what may, knowing that God had my back.

• **(L)** Communicate.   Don't be afraid to verbally acknowledge where you are in the transition. Those who love and understand you will walk with you and help you. Keeping Niya in the know helped us tremendously. Asking her opinion caused her to think logically, which is a skill we all need to embrace. Once I saw that she too had been blessed with wisdom, I started asking her about more things and gaining insight and a perspective that I might not have had. Parents, even though you have the final say, your children will appreciate being included. Include them in your decisions, they'll include you in theirs.

• **(L)** Don't settle because the end is not in sight.   Hold on to what you know God is doing. Do not allow the fear of what people will say about you push you to make a premature decision. I actually had someone call me (in deep and hushed tone) to tell me that I should not be out here in these streets "uncovered." Did they not know that a God who does everything decently and in order would have instructed me to be the same, therefore, He caused me to enter into pastoral care? God's sheep know His voice and another they will not follow. Many will speak but their words are all silenced as God is glorified in your life. Stay the course. Settling is not in your vocabulary.

• **(L)** Don't be afraid of change.   People who subscribe to doing the same thing, the same way, at the same time, for the same reasons will not evolve. Yes, GG Mama may have started the tradition 100 years ago and everyone in your family has since followed suit. That's awesome. However, if God is showing you a new way that will work

45

best for you, your family, and what He has ordained for you to do, don't you dare be afraid to go with it. Thankfully, none of us are an island to ourselves. We mature and gain inspiration from others. However, inspiration and dictation are different things. The "If ain't broke, then don't try to fix it" mentality can oftentimes be flawed. By whose definition of "broke" are we basing our decisions to fix or not to fix things off of anyway? I'll go with God for the win Alex.

- **(S)** Teenagers, remember that you can talk to your parents about anything no matter how scary, unfair or maybe even embarrassing the situation might be. No one should go through a transition alone. Like I said earlier, talking to my mom helped me to understand the decisions she made. Although I did not agree at the time, I understood and that helped me evolve. The truth is that I may not want to tell my mom everything and that's okay but eventually I will tell her. I just pray that she doesn't get mad that I held the truth for however long I chose to hold it. LOL!

- **(S)** Parents, understanding your teen and what they are going through (their thoughts and feelings) in transitions as well as being supportive while still being encouraging is something that you must do. When parents do not help their teens, the transition is harder and the teenager will not handle things the right way. They may even become lost. I know that my emotions, logic and thoughts get all mixed up and I need support. In these moments, I have to know that someone is there for me.

- **(S)** Teenagers, when transitioning into new places, don't worry about how many friends you have. Be you and keep an open eye for people that you haven't talked to as much. You might find a great friend in them. If you keep focusing on what you don't have, you'll miss all you do have. If God gives you one good friend, thank Him for that and keep going on with life.

- **(BOTH)** Enjoy the transition. It's just another stop on your journey. Aren't you glad you have someone along for the ride?

Prayer

Father we love you. We approach your throne of grace humbly, transparent about the terror of our transitions. We need you right now. You have not given us the spirit of fear, yet if we're honest, fear for some of us is lurking in the background, attempting to attach itself to us at our weakest moments. Some of us, God, are at the point of losing our minds because we are watching what appears to be everything that we have lived for, worked for, sacrificed for, and believed in slip through our very hands. We are confused because we are battling in our thoughts as to whether this is you, and if it is, we can't understand why. Our eyes are so full of tears God that we cannot see clearly. We question if we are going through a "Job experience" or are we justly paying for something that we did or did not do. Either way, we are in trouble.

God! Step in. You are not the author of confusion. You do not give us more than what we are able to bare. Let us see your goodness in the land of the living. Keep our feet from slipping. Let us worship you in this moment because we know that there is a time and season and a purpose under the heaven for everything. Though this valley seems full of shadows, help us to fear no evil, for you are with us. Your rod and your staff, they comfort us. Surround us with people that you have ordained to help us weather the changes we are experiencing. Help us to remain focused on the greater that is coming. Help us to submit to the truth that time and chance happens to us all. We know that we'll always have a better chance staying aligned with you. Help us to lift our hands, hearts, minds, and our will to you. Give us a genuine "nevertheless, not my will but yours be done." For thine is the kingdom, and the power and the glory, forever.

In Jesus name we pray, Amen.

Bonus: Niya and I chose the same scripture **(Proverbs 3:5-6)** as a reference for this chapter. It was not planned. See parents, they listen. It's in them. Keep planting the seeds!

4

Talk to Me, Baby!

Madre

I knew early on that communication was going to be an artform for Niya and I. Niya talked all day, every day. Before she could formulate words, she held full conversations by using a mixture of sounds, vowels and consonants that only the Spirit could interpret. I would laugh and act as if I understood her. This would excite her even more; so much so that the babble would continue. As she grew, Niya sought my approval for almost everything she said. She would say things like, "The sky is blue, right mom?" Or, "I'm a big girl now, right mom?" Or, "That was a bad thing to do, right mom?"

SWNM Niya: Mom. How many times are you gonna tell this story?! LOL!

SWNM MarQuita: FOR-EV-ER!

Again, I'd smile most affectionately co-signing her thoughts. Driving and listening to music was something that I've always loved to do. It was my time to retreat and unwind. Well, the begottens arrival changed all of that.

Car time became the appointed time for Niya to talk the most. At some point, I refrained from turning the music on at all. Don't get me wrong. I liked that my child enjoyed communicating with me. I really did. But since I made the decision to have her accompany me wherever I went 99.9% of the time, she talked 99% of the time. Her vocabulary grew rapidly because she was always around adults. ALWAYS. There'd be a room full of singers and musicians in a rehearsal and Niya. Sister circle book club and Niya. Shopping spree weekend with Niya. Colonics and Niya. That is, until Niya could fully understand the words that I used to be able to spell to keep from saying, or when she began to repeat the conversations that I had. I'm telling you! Niya's thought processes and her ability to communicate was well beyond her years; which was a blessing and a curse. At that point, we needed plan B (babysitter).

Now that my daughter is a teenager, our communication has shifted just a little bit. It (more frequently than I'd like) goes a little something like this:

What I said: "Niya, I need this thing (insert road map, photos and definition of the task) done by tonight at 7PM sharp. Here are the specific instructions to aid you in accomplishing the task at hand. There are no exceptions to my expectations. Do you understand?"

What she answered in the moment: "Yes."

What she obviously heard: "Niya, I need this thing done (or maybe I don't) at a time that is most convenient for you. You will suffer no repercussions should you choose to ignore my instructions (or better yet my humble request) because I am totally on your schedule, your will is what I want, and really, that's all that matters."

Wait. What? Weren't we just in the same conversation a second ago? How can I clearly hear the words that are coming out of my mouth at the exact time that you hear them yet you tell me that I've never said what I know I've said? Which one of us need to get our ears checked?

SWNM Niya: *Extreme side eye*

How are we in the same household, but speaking different languages?

49

In the above referenced example, my daughter and I were not speaking different languages at all. The offspring was simply being disobedient. However, there are times when what I say is honestly misinterpreted and misunderstood, and vice versa.

SWNM Niya: *I just need to add something. Mom, sometimes you say things in your head that you think you've said out loud!*

SWNM MarQuita: *I'd like to disagree but there's a strong possibility that you are correct.*

At times, in spite of my greatest efforts, I completely fail to decipher Niya-nese. I mean, I am totally clueless. Our wires are so crossed that I cannot tell where one starts and the other ends. In these moments, my heart literally sinks because I feel like I'm failing. I want so much to understand exactly what she's saying every time she speaks so she'll always want to talk with me and never choose to shut down. (The pressure is real.)

At times, I can see the frustration in her face as she attempts to communicate her point of view so I'll go ahead, take a chance and ask, "Can you repeat that?" Sometimes that works and sometimes it magnifies the frustration even more. All I know is that I've had to stop and ask myself what is it that is making what I say different from what is being received? Where is the disconnect? Of course, the solutions that immediately came to my mind were very basic. Maybe I just really failed at speaking clearly. Maybe my thoughts were not well formulated in my mind before I tried to share them with her.

Really, how can I expect for someone else to understand what I cannot appropriately articulate? Sounded good, but I knew there was more to it. I kept thinking, "Maybe you both were in a bad space at the moment." Could that be it? Maybe there were too many other things in Niya's mind that she felt were more important than what I was giving at the moment. *Shrugs* I began to settle into the, "Yeah, that must be its" and then it hit me. MarQuita, a large part of what you are dealing with lies in the differences found in listening versus hearing.

Jesus spoke to this in **Matthew 13:13** "This is why I speak to them in parables, because seeing they do not see, and hearing they do not hear, nor do they understand."

Placing myself in Niya's position, I came to this conclusion: It can be very intimidating as a child to stand eyeball to eyeball with your mother in those not so pleasant moments. I'm pretty tall (she's taller than me now), I'm bold and bright (her bold and bright is increasing everyday), I say what I mean and mean exactly what I say, and my very presence and my mouth can be quite big. I get it. I am the law of the land for the most part when it comes to her coming and going for now. She does not want to disappoint me, nor does she want to reveal things that may make her feel ashamed, but THAT IS WHAT I'M HERE FOR.

SWNM Niya: Nice to know!

I never want her to feel anything but support, so I express to her that there is absolutely nothing that she can do or say that will ever make me not love her, give up on her, disown her or push her away. Nothing. Still there's crickets. No facial expression, no emotion, nothing. *★Taps mic★* Is this thing on? In these times, I feel like my Savior, "Seeing, you don't see. Hearing, you don't hear." If I'm not careful, this is followed by a reactive attitude on my part of, "Go to your room, give me my phone, don't you turn on the television, straighten up your face little girl."

SWNM Niya: The classics.

Is God pleased with that? No. He is not.

Beloved, the primary function of our ears is to hear and process a vast array of sound. That sound is transferred into electrical energy that signals the brain. The brain then interprets the sound. Our ears aid us in keeping our balance. (Yes, it's true.) Those of us blessed with fully functioning ears will hear things whether we want to or not. We will not have to try. It naturally happens. Listening, however, takes hearing to another level.

In order to listen, I must make a conscious decision to circumvent my ears natural functioning in order to block everything or everyone else out in an effort to be fully invested in whatever is being discussed at the moment. Listening requires work; *a lot* of work. Active listening is an art where the receiver repeats what they've heard the communicator say in an effort to ensure that what they've heard the communicator actually said. It also allows the receiver to reinforce to the communicator that they are invested in what is being communicated. It's says, "Hey, you matter." Active listening with teenagers can become nagging and irritating at times. (Yeah, I said it!) Some will not see the beauty in your attempt to focus in on them, because they actually want the focus off of them depending on what you are talking about. Instead of saying, "Wow mom, I appreciate this moment of reflection", it can become "Mom, I just said that" or "Mom, I already know that" or the crickets... the crickets will return.

When I'm listening to Niya I am seeking to understand her. There's more than just my ears working at this point. My mind should be awakened and my heart should be opened to receive whatever she is trying to say to me. Yes, ultimately the goal is to get to the "bottom line" in an effort to reach an end resolve. This will only happen when I truly understand why her bottom line (the point that she is trying to make or get across to me) is the bottom line for her in the first place. The word of God sums it up this way, "The beginning of wisdom is this: Get wisdom, and whatever you get, get insight." **Proverbs 4:7** Hear me, please. Let those ears function, but as they function, engage the other parts of you and listen to what you are hearing so there can be positive and effective forward movement.

A person's body language and their unique personality also play major roles in how they communicate. A person who is animated (guilty as charged) will probably give you widened or lowered eyebrows, a plethora of hand gestures, and raised voices and sounds where you may actually need an interpreter to understand and Jesus to keep you out of your feelings. We mean you no harm. We're simply communicating. In doing so, you are going to feel every emotion that we feel. You may even get tapped a time or two. Don't you worry about it, you're safe. Why? We are simply communicating.

A person who is more reserved may not give you as much. You may find them more difficult to read. They may have what appears to be a blank stare. At times, you may feel that they are disconnected or even disinterested in what you are trying to convey, all of which may be inaccurate assumptions. People who are polar opposites on the communication spectrum need to be extremely aware of this, particularly when attempting to foster healthy parent/child relationships. Niya and I are so much alike, yet we are equally different. There's another set of genes at work here. There's an entire set of experiences at work here (hers). Parents, isn't it crazy how your child can be all you, all them, and all of the other parent at the same time? I promise you it's true. Niya can be very controlled when it comes to responding to stimuli from the outside. That control can come across as her being extremely nonchalant. That nonchalant attitude displays instantly on her face. The nonchalant attitude is not me. The "wearing whatever I'm feeling on my face" is **ME** (we are both working on improving in this area.) If we're happy, you'll know it, mad you'll know it, uninterested, you'll know it instantaneously. We care enough for you to know that we care. The operative word that comes before it is what is concerning (the **do** care or **do not** care.)

Dominant traits are developed based on the time one spends in the dominant environment. I've had to learn (and at times I'm still learning) to pause and tune into myself. I ask myself, "MarQuita, are you power tripping? Are you being super sensitive because she's not communicating or reacting to your communication in a way that you feel she should?" If the answer is yes, I try my best to redirect this displaced emotion. If the answer is no, then the internal questioning is more along the lines of, "MarQuita, are you witnessing signs of disrespect that need to be corrected quick fast and in a hurry"? If no, we sit down and we talk until we get to the root of the problem regardless of the time it takes to reach an understanding. If yes, we govern ourselves accordingly.

Riddle me this: What do parents believe will be accomplished when our reply to our children is "because I said so?" Yes, there are times when you give a directive that your children will simply have to follow. As a matter of fact, I have a perfect example for you. Niya and I returned home after a long day out. As I parked the car, we both started to clear the bags, making several trips. During one of these trips, Niya crossed the street, neglecting to look both ways. I looked up because I could hear a car speeding down to the bottom of the hill (which is right where we were). I was too far away from Niya to be able to get to her, so I immediately yelled, "Run across the street." Niya stopped walking to turn around to look at me. I yelled at her again, "Girl, run now!" Once she saw the emotion in my face, she took off! The car was seconds from reaching her. Our hearts were beating out of our chests.

Once we were safe in our home, we processed the experience. If Niya had waited a second longer, she would have been hit and possibly killed by the speeding car. I told her that, although I understood that she only stopped to gain more clarity in the moment, sometimes she just has to move when I say move. I'm looking when she's not looking. I'm praying about things and she is unaware. I've cleared paths before she arrives to them. Here's some truth parents: Your child's ability to trust you to move just because "you said so" comes because you've fostered an atmosphere of trust within your home when you didn't have to say a word. If you make a promise (no matter how large or small), keep your word. If you set discipline, even when it hurts you to do so, follow through. If you set the rules of the house, you must abide by them also.

Teenagers are much closer to being adults than newborns. I'm sure most parents would frown at the thought of having to bathe, brush the teeth of, and burp their 15-year-olds. If you frown at that, you should also frown at the thought of raising a child who must come to you before they can make any intelligent decision, a child who cannot control their own emotions, and cannot verbalize what is or is not good for them. I do. I give Niya permission to ask questions regarding rules and regulations or decisions that I make. It's important to me that while

I still have influence that I model good decision practices, integrity, honor, common sense, and the like. It is rare that my response to her is simply, "because I said so." Remember, I understand that everything I do is preparing her to live **without** me.

If I want my child to be successful in relationships outside of ours, I need to walk through the process of learning how to communicate with her. How will she be able to share her needs and feelings to a potential mate, her friends, or an employer if I do not teach her how? How will she learn to communicate the heart of God to the people she needs to if I do not show her how? I have to be wise enough and vulnerable enough to do so, especially in those moments where we have differing opinions. It is important to me to lay a foundation with her where she, within her treasured relationships, fosters the process of reconciliation. In other words, I want her to be able to facilitate understanding.

If ever she is found in conflict with another, I want Niya to be able to be the voice of reason that says that we (all parties involved) cannot get up from here (physically, spiritually, mentally, emotionally) until this (whatever it is) is settled. One of the greatest conversations I've ever had in my life started as a disagreement that I was having with my father. I was around the age of 11 when my dad called me to explain that he and my mother were going to be divorced. I was totally hurt, and a whole lot of angry. In my little mind, this was unacceptable and I was going to defend my mother. I "called" myself telling him exactly how I felt about him which wasn't nice (totally contrary to my upbringing). My mother was in the kitchen cooking. I remember going downstairs to tell her what happened, waiting for her to smile in agreement. She absolutely did not agree. Her words still replay in my mind to this day. "Call your father back and apologize to him for your behavior." What? Wait. Huh? Apologize? For my behavior? Why would I do that? My mother saw the confusion on my face and repeated herself. "Call your father and apologize." I walked up the stairs to my bedroom angry. It took me a minute, but I called my dad. When he answered, I was such a ball of emotions to the point where I could not speak. Finally, I whispered through tears, "Daddy, I'm sorry for being disrespectful." He replied, "I understand MarQuita. Do you want to talk about it?" My father allowed me to say everything that I needed to say in that moment. He allowed me to ask everything that I needed to ask in that moment. This conversation sparked the super close, open relationship that I had with him until his death. It built faith that I could really talk to my father about anything when he allowed me to bare my soul regarding what was so hurtful to me which at that moment was him.

I talked to my mother every day. Our relationship was different. I knew I could talk to her but I really didn't share as much as I'm sure she would have liked me to. Mom was the constant authority. She was the preacher. A conversation with her seemed to always lead to, "Well what did Jesus say?" That wasn't a bad thing; however, sometimes I would tell her, "I just need my mom right now, not the preacher." I'm older now. Our communication has changed because our relationship has changed. I'm very clear that she will forever be my mother and I respect her as such. However, she's my mother/homie. She's Mom Dukes, The Dukes, and at times Listen Here Lady. The greatest part about our relationship now is that when I choose to call her (or she calls me), I can disconnect the phone and end the conversation when I'm good and ready. *Right mom?* Lol! Remember when you told me that when I get old and get my own phone I can do with it whatever I'd like? (No? You don't remember that? Yes, you did!) LOL!

SWNM Niya: And you said it to me too! Just be ready!

Seriously, at the end of the day, I want meaningful relationships. I try my best to remember: "For no good tree bears bad fruit, nor again does a bad tree bear good fruit, for each tree is known by its own fruit. For figs are not gathered from thorn bushes, nor are grapes picked from a bramble bush. The good person out of the good treasure of his heart produces good, and the evil person out of the evil treasure produces evil, for out of the abundance of the heart his mouth speaks." **Luke 6:43-45** My mouth will speak what is in my heart. With that in mind, I've decided to not only hear but listen, commit myself to making things right when they are wrong and bringing restoration in a spirit of meekness, considering the times that I have failed and will fail. I understand that I can't always communicate at the time that I may feel that I need to, but I know for the sake of love, it's worth the wait. Sometimes when we shut up, God can speak up, and we'll see that what we thought we needed to say was not as important than the need to simply pray.

Hija

"But avoid irreverent (having a lack of respect) babble, for it will lead people into more and more ungodliness..." **2 Timothy 2:16**

To communicate is to be successful in sharing ideas and feelings. The secondary meaning of the word "communication" is a connection between people. Open communication between a mother and a daughter can really benefit their relationship as well as their individual lives. Both can live happily, knowing that they have a trust and confidence with one another. You need this. After all, you are stuck with each other for a very longggg time! LOL! This communication should be more than just the act of talking. It should be talking with the intentions of reaching a complete understanding. Communication should be comfortable because you know that what is being said comes from a place of love.

I've learned a few things about constructive criticism and how that must be communicated and received. I've also learned that there is a **BIG** difference between constructive criticism and someone just being mean. Here's an example: If a friend of mine is wearing something unappealing, as a friend I should be able to say, "I don't think your outfit looks good on you. You should maybe try something else." My intention is to help. If I wanted to be mean I would simply say, "You look terrible" and leave it there with no explanation. If my friend smells badly (just giving another example), I would want to be the person to tell her, rather than someone with evil intentions.

At times, my mom has said things that she thought was supportive but what she said actually upset me more. In my opinion, the words just came out all wrong. I do believe that if you are talking with someone you really love, you should tell them the truth, but you should be careful of what and how you say things. In the end, if you come across harsh when you try to help, you'll always seem mean. Now teenagers, it's safe to say that 99 percent of the time your mom is just trying to help you because she loves you. People who really love you will tell you if what you are doing is right or wrong. Moms, please don't forget that we are still human and will make mistakes sometimes. Teens, let's be honest, we can be very sensitive with receiving words of instruction or direction when it's not what we want to hear. It is what we need to hear, so we have to be careful of how we react to things.

SWNM MarQuita: *Revelation!*

When communicating is hard for me, I really try to stop and comprehend where the other person is coming from. Here's an example: I can be really lazy sometimes and will not want to do my schoolwork or my house chores. My mom and I will get into a disagreement. Most of the time she's right, but sometimes I feel as if she feels she's always right when she's not and it makes it hard for me to hide my temper having that thought in the back of my mind.

SWNM MarQuita: *Did you all read that? She said most of the times I am RIGHT! Nothing behind the "but" matters. LOL! Oh, bless Him!*

I know that I'm not always going to be the one that's always right, and she's not always going to be the one that's always wrong. I acknowledge that and I hope she understands that I acknowledge that. (I don't think she does sometimes).

SWNM MarQuita: *I do babycakes.*

I may not show emotion when we're talking, but I am listening. I just don't want to show anything that will make the situation worse. In my mind, the best thing for me to do is to keep my feelings inside and pray that eventually they will go away. Once I realized that's never going to happen, I became okay with having to communicate to figure things out. Then there are times that I don't want to tell my mom what's wrong because I'll get into trouble. For example, if I am upset that I didn't get a shirt or pair of shoes I wanted, I am going to be upset. I might stop talking for a little or just put my headphones in. My mom will ask me what's wrong. If I tell her, I might get hit with the, "You should be grateful for what you already have" card. It's not that I'm ungrateful. No. I'm simply disappointed because I wanted that shirt at that time.

Is it okay to show emotion? We have to. Moms, please don't get mad when we show some emotion and if we share our feelings. It makes teens not want to talk or communicate. On the other hand, teens we should know that sometimes we (yes, we) are being spoiled and selfish. It may be hard for our moms to get what they give us in the first place and we should appreciate this more.

Some mothers may not know where to start when trying to communicate with their daughters. I think I can speak for most teenage girls when I say that there are times when mothers will just need to give their teenagers some space.

SWNM MarQuita: Oh! This is being said by the person who will, without warning, jump into my bed regardless of how I feel, snuggle her entire head in between my chin and my chest, sets up her living quarters in my room when she has her own...I can go on, but I won't. Space? Tuh!

Truth is that after my mom and I have a disagreement, sometimes I just need time alone to be able to retreat and think by myself without anyone judging me because of my thoughts. That's not something she always gives me.

SWNM MarQuita: Working on it!

Forcing us to talk about something (unless it's a life or death situation) will only make things worse. I will eventually realize that what I did was wrong and talk to her about it. In reality, teens should not get upset about some things in the first place. We must learn how to control our emotions. When my mom and I have our talks after a disagreement or misunderstanding she usually asks me what I'm feeling. When I tell her, that makes things a little better than it was before. I still receive correction for my actions but at least she understands why I did what I did. I've also found that good communication can even lighten up the consequences. It's like once we come together and talk about the problem things get better. The best thing is that at the end of it all we pray and hug it out. Things are alright after that.

Some teens are easier to understand and guide than others, because they may be comfortable with opening up and talking about their feelings. Not all are like that. Teens can be easily embarrassed when they have a problem but they don't know how to fix it on their own. I have experienced this. I know how it feels not wanting to ask your mom about something that was going on with your body because she'll give you a whole speech. (You know how preachers do. Just get ready.) As a teenager, I understand not wanting to embarrass yourself by sharing a problem but if it's important to you, and you don't talk to someone, then the problem may get worse. You never know, your mom might have already gone through what you are going through and could help you a lot more than you think. The best person to talk to, in most situations, is your mom. She has already overcome the things you are struggling with and can give you advice on what you should do. (After trying this myself, I realized that moms aren't that bad after all! Well they can be but...)

SWNM MarQuita: *Ha!*

Try this. Go to your mom and say, "Mom, can you help me with something?" or "Mom, I need your advice." You probably won't hear, "Nope. Sorry I don't feel like helping you today." She'll be there for you immediately. This is something that I love about moms in general. It doesn't even have to be your mom! Moms are so easy to communicate with (most of the time). I remember telling my mom about a problem that I was having while she was doing my hair. She helped me alot and made my life so much easier (not that it was THAT hard in the first place). Trust me. If you just talk and communicate with your mom your relationship will prosper. Parents, just make sure that you always remind your child that they can talk to you about anything. That may help them open up to you more.

This is how we do it:

- **(M)** Create what I'd like to call your communication evacuation plans prior to needing them. You cannot wait until things are going downhill to set up the rules for proper communication in your home. That's like waiting until the first snowflake literally falls from the sky before you plan to go to the supermarket to buy groceries, or waiting to buy snow salt after hearing that there's a possible 12-21 inches of snow expected to fall within the next 24 hours. We don't play with that over here on the East Coast/Tri-state area. As sure as you are alive at this moment, you will face disagreements while trying to communicate with others - and that's ok. Acknowledge that space. Own it. But refuse to remain there together. Your trusty plan is there to assist!

- **(M)** As part of our communication evacuation plan, we've established and force ourselves with all of our might to comply with the "no grudge zone." Have you ever been in a heated argument or a very emotional conversation with someone and once it's over you remembered all of the things that you *should* have said? Have you ever tried to articulate your feelings but the environment at that time was not conducive? I have. I've found that most times, the things I failed to vocalize in that moment were paramount. You know what I mean! These are the things that lay on your heart and your mind so much that you go to bed thinking about it, wake up in the morning thinking about it, travel to school or work talking to your friends about it, chew over it while chewing your food at dinner, looking for a way to say, "We need to talk." These are normally the things that we need the other person to not only hear but understand so our relationship can remain intact (unless we are just being petty). A particular situation may have brought these feeling to the surface, but the real issue is so much bigger than what is currently being dealt with. These are things that need to be released because they have been mounting up for a considerable amount of time and so, to prevent either party from catching a case from kicking someone in the throat, these things need to get out, and now.

So here are the rules: When either of us get to a place where we need to talk but we know that we can't quite do it right now without tempers, feelings, emotions and the like completely flaring up and things ending badly, we use the evacuation plan with the no grudge zone benefit. No grudge means that both parties must keep a completely open heart, check attitudes at the door, and must refrain from making any decisions or judgment calls before going through the communication process. (Please note: the circumstance must meet all the guidelines to determine if it is no grudge zone eligible. LOL!) A certain amount of time is given for the requester to go through their own process and bring it to the other person. If you cannot get to a total place of understanding, additional time is given to revisit the situation. If you get to a place of understanding, a set amount of time is still given to revisit the situation just in case there were some things left unsaid or unexplored. (The time frame varies depending on the nature of the situation.). Once it's done, it's done, over, finished. The end. It doesn't always go as smoothly as it reads, however, remembering it most certainly helps.

Some may not agree with this format because to them it appears that it leaves an open door to consistently revisit a wound with no point of resolution. It is actually the opposite for us, so *for now it is safe*. We are both deep thinkers. We replay things over and over again in our minds. I know this of myself and my child. If I set a rule in my home that prevents healthy dialogue with a life entrusted to me swiftly heading to adulthood, I will actually do more harm than good. If you're up for it, try it. Set the ground rules from the very beginning and try to ensure that everyone equally buys into the process. At the end of the day, if my focus is peace and healing, I'm going to avail myself to walk through the process with you, and you with me. With God invited, we really can reason together, our bond is strengthened and we can move on- until the next time.

- **(M)** Revise the plan when necessary. I cannot stress this enough. Parents, you must constantly reevaluate your processes of how you are raising your children as you both mature. What you set for today may not work as they get older. Truth is, some things should not! Think about it this way: Our physical bodies show us that as it gets older it requires a different level of attention, maintenance, and a revision on what we believe is safe enough to allow into it or expose it to. Revision does not mean that what you set up has failed. Revision means you're wise enough to know that the eraser on a pencil is there for a reason. Pride will keep you stuck somewhere where God has provided a way of escape.

- **(M)** Acknowledge your child's transitions and how they will affect their level of communication. Be honest about who you both are, where you both need to be, and what it will take to get there. Consider things such as temperament, personalities, experiences etc., and set yourselves up to survive the awkward moments where everyone wants to talk, but no one is listening (or vice versa). If it hasn't happened yet, get ready. I'll tell you what my mom would say to you, "Keep living." It, much like your blessing, is on the way!

- **(M)** Watch B.E.T. (body language, excuses, tone).

SWNM Niya: Mom, that acronym is wrong. It should be B.L.E.T. You can't leave out the "l" for language.

SWNM MarQuita: Nope. I like B.E.T. Readers, you can decide whatever acronym you want to use; just get the point.

I can say the most beautiful words out of my mouth, but if my face is mean and unwelcoming, my lips are tight, and my eyes are rolling, the beauty quickly fades and the person on the other side of the conversation has already concluded that our conversation is a waste of time. Watch your *body language*. While communicating with someone else, my words and my actions should be one in the same. My posture should be one that shows that I am attentive and purposefully here in this moment with you. My eyes should be fixated on you.

While communicating (especially about the hard stuff), I have to consciously remove all of the *excuses* that will creep up within me that I could use to explain why I've handled things the way that I have because they have become a part of my "personality." These excuses will hinder the success of our communication. If I'm wrong, I'm wrong. "That's just the way that I am" will keep you just the way that you are. "That's what I was taught" will limit you because in their best efforts, no parent can teach you everything. If you were raised in the home where your parents physically fought and cursed at each other and it damaged you, why would you want that for your children? Break the comfort found in excuses that make it easy for you to not have to put in work and just become better. Watch your *tone*. Believe it or not, the tone and pitch in your voice matters when communicating with others. The Bible is clear in **Proverbs 15:1** "A soft answers turn away wrath, but a harsh word stirs up anger." What do you expect to accomplish growling at people? Not much.

- **(H)** Moms, when talking to your daughter and it seems like she is being rebellious by not wanting to talk, she may just need space. You should give it to her and not get angered by the silence. Sometimes, I just don't want to talk about somethings. I would rather keep them to myself. For me, I'm not going to keep something big from my mom but I'm not going to tell her EVERYTHING. I don't think there's anything wrong with keeping somethings from my mom. She might disagree but hey, I'm pretty sure she didn't tell my grandma everything. LOL! The funny thing about space is that although you need to give it to us, you still need to be present. If you are not, it may seem like you don't care. (Crazy, right?) The other thing is that sometimes experiences can hurt somebody so much that they don't want to speak about it. Forcing them could just make the situation worse. For me, when I'm quiet, I am just working things out in my head. My mom sometimes will say, "Why do you have an attitude?" and I'll say, "I don't." By the end of the conversation, I end up with an attitude because I'm constantly saying that I didn't have an attitude to begin with. Ironic I know, but this particular situation happens a lot right now. We're working on it.

- **(H)** Moms, if you're going to ask us what's wrong please don't get mad or start yelling if we actually start to tell you what's wrong. It just makes us not want to tell you anything. I know I still don't tell my mom what is actually wrong at times just because I know what her reaction will be. Or at least I think I do.

SWNM MarQuita: Right. You think you do.

Sometimes I feel it's better for me to keep it in, and I'm right. Sometimes I'm not. At the same time teens, make sure to watch your **"B.L. E.T."** After all your mom is still your mom. There will be times when one or both of you will overreact so you want to make sure you handle each situation carefully.

Prayer

Hello God. What a privilege and an honor to be able to talk to you. You are mindful of us, and we are grateful. Our prayer today is that you help us effectively communicate with each other. We first acknowledge that you have given us prayer as a tool of communication with you. We thank you for your spirit that makes intercession for us when we do not know what we should pray for. We know that the more we pray the more power and instruction we receive. Download Your will into us, Oh God. Increase our prayer time. Increase our desire to communicate with you. Increase our desire to communicate with each other. Give us the right words to say and the right time in which to say them. Let our mouths speak words of life, encouragement, validation, respect, and love. Let our words release each other from any feelings of anxiety, inadequacy and defeat. Help us to foster safety in the spirits of our loved ones. Lord, our children need to know that we, their parents, are constant. We will not waver in our positive reinforcement. We will not waiver in our correction. We will not waiver in intentionally finding ways to remain on the same page. We are opened to learning the skills we need to raise your amazing disciples. The discipleship begins in our homes. Let us acknowledge our differences and see those differences as the blessings that they are. Lord, our parents need to feel appreciated for all of their hard work. Help us to be humble to their leadership. Help us to support their decisions, even if we do not understand them. Help us to bring our parents joy and not pain. Help us God. We know that we are never alone, therefore we do not have to deal with our thoughts and feelings alone. Let our words be seasoned with grace. Let the words of our mouth and the meditation of our hearts be acceptable in your sight. Let us go beyond just hearing. Teach us how to effectively listen and give us the ability to take the proper course of action. We thank you, we praise you, and we count it done.

In Jesus name we pray, Amen.

5

Divas Aren't Made
Overnight, Child!

Big Diva

I know. I know. There are so many negative definitions of the word
"diva" floating around that we question if our being defined as one is a
good or a bad thing. In our home, Niya and I have chosen to embrace a
portion of the true definition of the word that speaks to the diva being
the premier performer (a person who entertains an audience, as in an
opera or in the theatre). The diva is the famous one.

The word diva has followed me for a very long time. It has been given
to me as a nickname by my friends, by strangers who have had one
encounter with me, and is a part of my line name. I finally decided to
accept it, pass it down to my daughter, and use it as a way to remain
focused, not to boast or brag about accomplishments. For us, it stands
as a reminder of the excellence that we should pursue, to remind us
that we should strive to always be premier (best, important, leading),
and to remind us that we need to do all things so well that we are
famous (noted, excellent, noteworthy, celebrated) for it. To perform
(accomplish, fulfill, carry out), one must take action. It is understood
that in our home we are to carry out and accomplish our goals, dreams,
and assignments with the absolute best of our abilities, so much so that
excellence will be our legacy/testimony. The most important part of

this diva mentality is that it is not for the sake of receiving glory from man, but to give glory to God. Ultimately, He is the intended audience for whom we perform.

Friends, with the world as your stage, the spotlight is always on you. People are watching what we do, listening to what we say, discussing our personal choices in everything from clothing to the company that we keep, and oftentimes using our journey to help to create their own. What we display directly affects the Kingdom of God. We are, after all, light. We are a city on a hill that cannot be hid. We have to find the way to be the light and the city while enjoying living through this human experience. Each of us were given the exact shape, height, eye color, hair texture, smile and personality necessary to accomplish our missions. Since we are going to be seen, and since we have to shine, let's do it and do it BIG (and look right while we're doing it).

My mother is a straight up southern belle. She's very dainty, very well put together. She taught my brother and I to have pride in ourselves and in our appearance whenever we presented ourselves to the outside world. It seems to be the norm today, but we would have never been allowed to go outside in the clothes that we slept in growing up in Iola's house. We would have never been able to go outside with a non-fashion scarf or do-rag on our heads. We would have never been allowed to go outside without brushing our teeth, combing our hair, or washing our bodies. NEVER! Our appearance was a reflection of our mother and she wanted (as she should) people to see that her children were being raised to be great, respectable, wholesome and clean (inside and out). I appreciate my mother's conviction. Because of it, I do not allow Niya to leave the house (as mom would say) "any ole' kind of way!" "Iron your clothes!" "Adjust them to fit properly on your body!" "Wear tights under your skirt or pants for an extra layer of protection from the elements!" "Wear the right shoes on your feet!" "Where's your coat? Well put it on and button it up!" EVERY DAY. I find myself repeating this list every day. It should come as no surprise as my mother had to repeat this same list to Ray and I; especially the *where's your coat thing*.

We are what my mom likes to call "hot natured," meaning we are normally physically hot even when it's dangerously cold. During the winter, we would attempt to go outside without coats on or with the minimum amount of coverage that the weather would allow. To this she would exclaim, "Keep it up! Old man Arthur is going to settle in those bones."

SWNM Niya: Who's Arthur?

SWNM MarQuita: Uh, let me finish please.

As a child, I understood what she was saying, but never fully believed that Arthur (arthritis) would ever be my reality.

SWNM Niya: Ohhhh! Why didn't she just say, "You're going to get arthritis?"

SWNM MarQuita: Ask her.

SWNM Niya: No, no, no. Let's go with grandma and this old man thing.

SWNM MarQuita: LOL! Good call. She was right by the way!

Once I witnessed Old man Arthur become a constant member in the lives of others my age, I at least covered what I thought were the most important joints! Niya likes to leave the house in the winter without shoes that actually cover her feet. She prefers socks and flip flops.

SWNM Niya: ★Covers face with hand★ Slides mom. Slides are much cooler! Plus, they have good grip on the bottom!

Parents, did you gasp right there? You should have. It's a sight to behold. Naturally, my response is that of my mother. Without a thought (when I catch her), I yell out of the door as she walks away, "Keep it up. You're going to get sick. I'm not going to any hospitals, and you're still going to school." (My version of Arthur).

My mother had many skin care regimens and tips that she passed on to me. I must confess that her routines seemed a bit overbearing and unnecessary. I was young and vibrant! My skin was tight. My eyes were bright. Nothing was sagging at this point; yet she was adamant that I needed to incorporate everything that she was teaching me now. Natural remedies for facial cleansers and toners (lemons and honey), hair conditioners (milk and eggs) was what we did. She had what appeared to be the strangest way to cure a cold or break a fever using things like onions and potatoes wrapped in a piece of cloth. Go figure! Mom always stressed the importance of drinking water to flush out toxins, rejuvenate the skin and the organs, and for ladies to help to keep certain areas cleansed. Amen. Herbal tea leaves and medications for everything from the common cold to memory retention were the norm for us. Physical activities from swimming lessons to civil air patrol? Normal. Charm school for me? Normal. She was always sending us to a class or a seminar so that our learning was beyond the Bible and our studies in school. We learned about self-love and self-care. I remember my first "this is your body" book. It was quite amusing. I remember the encyclopedia of healthy foods and their uses. Mom was always on a journey for better, and we were along for the ride. Now that I am 41, I actually reap the benefits from putting into practice the tips that my mother shared with me as a child. I have been blessed with good health, great skin and hair, and a great functioning body. (Thank you, Jesus!)

SWNM Niya: *Amen! So have I.*

Good health is important. A good understanding of our responsibility to show the world that our God is good by how we take care of ourselves is also important. Who would want to serve a God whose children are all sick and dying? Not too many people.

I did not explore the wonderful world of makeup until I was older, like college older. Makeup was not really accepted at the church I attended as a child (let's start with that.) Growing up, we rocked moisturizer and the basic carmax or the real big wax lip glosses. The end. My intro to makeup began with eyeshadow and mascara. Lipstick soon followed.

Foundation and concealer was still far in the distance. Highlighters? What's that?! I always had a fear of looking like a clown, looking cheap or being unacceptable, until I realized that proper application of makeup should only enhance my already beautiful face not make me look like a totally different person. I could apply it, be sophisticated, acceptable, and Jesus would still love me! Once I found the liberty in this regard, I hit the ground running. I took the time to learn what products were best for my skin and how to appropriately apply them. Hooked!

Naturally my daughter began to become interested in makeup from watching me, so I'd let her play with my palettes in the house. She was surrounded by it more once she entered middle school. It appeared that it was normal for the young ladies attending her school to know how to apply full faces of makeup better than I did. During the 5th/6th grade, Niya wore small amounts of glitter and light-colored nail polish during special occasions. She was absolutely content with that, however, I could see the wheels turning in her head.

By the seventh grade, I knew that I had to make a decision. Either I am going to be intentional about letting her explore what she likes (which is a part of her natural journey towards maturation) while I can still carefully guide her hands and her decisions, or I can act like my "no" is going to stop her. It's not. She's still going to buy products (the wrong products). She'll probably hide them in her locker at school. Every day she'll leave home a little early as to give herself time to incorrectly apply these wrong products on her sensitive skin in the horribly lit school bathroom. She'll leave out of the bathroom looking like God ain't able; and we **KNOW** that He is.

SWNM Niya: *I choose choice #1. Let me explore while you're there to help me please.*

Think about it. She'd also have to try to perfectly wipe all of the evidence off before she gets home from school. That's disobedience, manipulation, and dishonesty. Why would I cause her little soul to have to make that decision? I decided that I was going to allow her to grow and be along for the journey. I gave her the best tips that I had. I laughed at her and all of the bloopers that came along with learning proper application techniques. Believe me, there were many! That was my decision. I was not, in any way, deterred by the people who thought my approach was incorrect at the moment. ***Shrugs.*** She's not your child.

Niya also became interested in all types of hair, hairstyles, hair accessories, and hair products. She is the definition of a product junkie and for good reason! Niya has watched as my hair has transformed in almost every length, every cut and in many colors. I've had the asymmetrical cuts, the super-tight rod sets, braids and faux locs, extremely long weaves, weave caps, natural afros...you name it!! The only process that I've never had to date was the curl. Mom Dukes wasn't having the drip in her house! LOL!

I was born with a beautiful head of very thick hair. When I allow it to grow, it's a very nice length. Operative word is *allow*. LOL! I truly believe that an important part of healthy self-discovery is healthy self-exploration. My hair has allowed me to express myself, and what I felt was the message that I wanted to send to the world at the moment. I've never been afraid to change it. My motto is, "It's hair! It'll grow back!"

Clothing has always been an extension of my inner creativity. At 41, I am very settled in my divaliciousness. What's "in" for me is what I make "in." I've tried to teach Niya that while it's quite alright to follow the fashion do's and don'ts, do not allow yourself to be confined by them. How about *you* be the person making the rules by simply being yourself! In time, I've learned how to take more costly pieces that I've paid what some may consider an extreme amount of money for and mix them with items that I've purchased from thrift or consignment shops and strut honey! You would never know which piece came from what place.

Let me pause to talk about thrifting for those who have concerns or issues with it. It's your right to have a concern or issue. I just want to give you something to ponder. I know you are very much aware that most of the clothes in your closets (depending on where you shop) have probably been on someone else's body right? Right! This happens for several reasons. To begin, we have this little thing called the dressing room where we try on clothing to determine whether we will purchase it or not. Have you ever wondered how many people have tried on that dress, that blouse, or better yet that bra that you just purchased before you? I wonder if they washed that day. Hmmm. Oh, but it doesn't stop there. There are people skilled in the ole' buy and return with tags trick. They purchase an item, take it to the club and shake a tail feather in it or wear it to church while praise dancing for Jesus only to return it to the store for a full refund.

SWNM Niya: *Shake a what now?!* **LOL!**

You come into the store, fall in love with the item and pay FULL price for it. It's used. It belonged to someone else. It was sweaty but they aired it out. This happens all of the time. Finding things that others have tossed away or no longer see as useful and remaking them into something brand new has proven to be very therapeutic for me. When I think of it, it so reminds me of what God did for me. He found me at the bottom of the last chance bin thrown in a corner at a going out of business rummage sale somewhere, blotted out the spots as He cleaned me up, straightened out my life as He stitched me back together, clothed me in royal garments with sparkles and then connected me to the people (pieces) that would make me the most beautiful masterpiece ever! (He's still doing that today).

Niya has been taught how extremely beautiful, lovely, and how fearfully and wonderfully made she is since she could hear in the womb. We have had in-depth conversations about things that would typically concern all women from our weight (an area that I've struggled with that I've never wanted her to have to struggle with) which leads into the conversations about the benefits of being healthy and fit versus simply being skinny for the sake of vanity, the acceptance of our body types and features, embracing our natural hair but being free enough to explore braids, weaves, wigs, colors and cuts. We've discussed that a person's use of coconut oil and all-natural products does not make them more "woke" to the perils of this world as an African American woman, just like a fresh perm does not make you better than those who choose to rock their natural curls. It's a matter of preference; a preference that you are free to have. Variety is a benefit that comes along with being a woman, and it should be celebrated!! The color of your skin, your race, ethnicity, and your culture is to be celebrated.

I find it interesting that women, a class who has had to fight and endure so much historically in this country, would ever find it necessary to segregate ourselves within ourselves with external things that are meaningless. Let's go back to hair for a second and use it as a topic of discussion here. (My example will reference African American women as I am one, but I'm sure it can serve as a point of reference for every race). There are women who've decided to wear their hair natural who actually believe that they are in some way better (by better I mean more in touch with their origin and roots, history, and the plight of the entire race) than women with chemically treated hair, more specifically perms. Yet these same women foster subdivisions within themselves where they believe that a fellow "natural sister" is not truly committed to the cause if she has any type of color or if she uses certain products in her hair. These women literally debate on social media posts about it all of the time in an effort to prove who's better and in an effort to distinguish that they are a little more real, authentic and pure. Can we just let people choose what they want for their lives? Who made you the guru of all things mother nature?

SWNM Niya: BURN!

SWNM MarQuita: Huh?

SWNM Niya: It's kinda like saying "She told you!"

SWNM MarQuita: Oh.

I don't have to walk around smelling like incense and shea butter to prove to others that I know who I am and that I appreciate who God has made me to be. When I wore my hair all naturale many *many* years ago (started with a big chop and allowed it to grow back to shoulder length), we did not have all of the youtube channels and products for our hair that are available today.

Additionally, choosing to wear your hair naturally at that time was not in any way as respected, praised or acceptable as it is today. I literally had older women and men ask me, "When are you going to do something with your hair?" Uhm. I did! It's done! It took me 2 hours to do it. Smh. On the flip side, there are women who choose the way of the "creamy crack" aka perms. Guess what? High five! Your choice. What offends me is when I see these women frown their faces at the woman or the young lady who has chosen to rock her beautiful natural tresses like it's an insult to "how far we've come."

I am offended by the woman who believes that this perm or this long weave will somehow disassociate her from being identified as an African American woman or those who use this hair as a cover up because inside they do not believe that their hair is good enough. I am concerned for those who believe that they are not beautiful unless their hair looks like the hair normally associated with other races, cultures and ethnicities. Listen here, you can perm your hair all you'd like but when those roots began to grow here comes Africa as bold, real and strong as ever! I love natural hair. I also love my perm. More than anything I love the freedom to decide and will teach my daughter that she has this freedom also.

The battle of the light-skinned woman versus the dark-skinned woman irks my entire soul. The battle of white is right (or wrong), down with brown and black is whack also irks my entire soul. It does. To keep this chapter from turning into something that it is not (a debate), I'll say a few things and move on.

In my humble opinion, no category of complexion (since we sum up an entire array of beautifully complected African American women into two categories) nor culture or race should ever feel like they have to fight for relevance. African American woman, God made you.

That means you are forever relevant! Women of other cultural, ethnic and racial backgrounds, God made you. That means you are forever relevant! Your body is simply an earthly tent to house your eternal spirit. God was showing off when He chose the different tones that He gave us. We are making ugly what He has made beautiful.

So stop. Breathe. I apologize to you for the tears you've cried when they made fun of you, demeaned you, or judged you solely based on the color of your skin and not the content of your character. I know that hurts. Please read what I'm saying to gain an understanding (and maybe some healing), not find a reason to protest. My skin is light. I had no choice in the matter but I love it. I equally love the skin of my chocolate Mommy. She's so pretty. When I look at her, I do not see her complexion. What I see is my nose. I see my smile. I see my mannerisms. That is beautiful to me. Our differences make us beautiful.

Can we eliminate all of the unnecessary comparisons? Big bottoms versus tiny bottoms. Big breast versus tiny breast. Big lips versus thin lips. Long eyelashes versus short eyelashes. Real eyebrows versus penciled eyebrows. Real hair versus fake hair. Tall versus short. Fat versus skinny. Can we stop? Our daughters would have better self images if we stopped force feeding them the ideas and images that insinuates that nothing that God gave them is good enough. They are good enough. Should they ever choose to enhance any part of themselves, they'll do it by way of choice not because we killed their spirits with our sickness. I get it. Our collective struggles were and are very real. So are our individual journeys. You still can never justify the need to tear another woman down through hateful words and actions. Never. We have to be the examples of what we want to see and experience in this world. I have to be the example of what I want to see within my daughter. If I do not want my daughter to struggle with her weight, I have to get my weight under control. I cannot bring family size bags of potato chips and multiple 2-liter sodas in the house. We cannot fry everything that we eat. If I want my daughter to be active, I have to show her the fun in playing outside (which is actually the best exercise ever). If I want my daughter to love her hair, I have to love mine. I must speak well of it, even when it does not do what I want it to do. If self-acceptance is the lesson, I have to love my face without makeup as much as I do when I wear it. I have to accept my big lips and the fact that my right foot is larger than my left. I have to learn to love the things that would be perfect about me in a perfect world if given a chance at perfection, understanding that that will never happen. I am imperfectly perfect, working hard to maintain what God gave me, improving on what I can. This is something we all have to embrace and teach our children.

Although we put our best foot forward in preserving and presenting our natural bodies, I am very clear to Niya that you cannot be beautiful on the outside and ugly on the inside. **Proverbs 31** tells us, "Charm can mislead and beauty soon fades. The woman to be admired and praised is the woman who lives in the Fear-of-God." We can perform and put on a great show to entertain an insignificant audience (remember our audience should be God and God alone) hidden behind loads of cosmetics, fancy clothing and with hair that sweeps the ground and it amounts to absolutely nothing.

The Bible is very clear that man looks on the outside appearances but God searches the heart. **I Samuel 16:7** The heart is what He is most concerned about. External beauty will never be able to compare to the true value of the internal. The most finest of things, the fairest of them all can live and be totally unfulfilled because inside they are corroded, ugly and full of hate for themselves and others. A woman who reverences God and respects Him (fears Him) shall be praised. As a young lady, I want my daughter to understand that her relationship with Christ is the most important thing that she will ever have. That relationship will teach her to honor her mind, body, spirit and soul. In honoring herself, she'll move in power and authority. She'll practice etiquette, she'll be clean, she'll understand that being able to cook and upkeep her physical space (and having a desire to want to own these skills) is noteworthy, and that being a lady is a must. My prayer is that Niya will truly understand the value of a good name. She'll know her worth, know her body and know her spirit. When she knows these things, she can demand respect from others. When she knows these things, she can give respect to others. I know this learning curve takes time, and she'll make mistakes along the way as every woman that has come before her has.

Understanding that you have divine purpose beyond your flaws is what makes a woman a true diva. Having the ability to walk through all that life will present with style and grace makes you an unforgettable premier performer. That alone will allow you to have influence beyond who you are. Be her; you Diva you!

Lil' Diva

"Or do you not know that your body is a temple of the Holy Spirit within you, whom you have from God? You are not your own, for you were bought with a price. So, glorify God in your body." **I Corinthians 6:19-20**

When I was a little girl, as far back as I can remember, I loved everything pretty, sparkly and mostly pink. My room was even pink and zebra print for awhile. I don't know why I liked pink, black and white so much but I did. Other little girls did too. There was just something so infatuating about the color combination. My mom taught me the word diva. I wasn't sure what it meant, but after she explained it to me it became the only word I used to describe myself. I define the word diva as a girl who is good at everything; makeup, styling clothes and hair. A diva is just lit in every category.

SWNM MarQuita: Define the word lit for the people who may not understand what it means please.

SWNM Niya: When something or someone is lit it is good, great, popping, turned up!

SWNM MarQuita: I see.

I was the ultimate diva in my mind because I had all of the pretty sparkly things. After awhile, I started caring more about my body and how I looked. This is when I was thrown into the world of makeup, hair, clothes, fitness, and taking care of myself.

Taking care of myself is a lot of work, especially because my mom has done everything for me for a very longgggggggg time. I had to learn how to cook, clean and all of that good stuff. By practicing, I'm learning what looks good on me and what does not. There are so many options when it comes to hair, clothing and makeup that you really just have to find what works for you and slay!

SWNM MarQuita: Niya, define the word slay for...never mind!

The downside of being a diva is the potential to have unnecessary pride. A person who knows that they look good or knows that they are talented, can sometimes become a little conceited. They'll find themselves dismissing the thoughts or suggestions from the people that they know really care about them. The response of a prideful person may sound something like, "I don't know who she thinks she's talking to. I look bomb. She can't tell me what to do." The prideful person may not say anything at all; but what they are thinking starts to show on their face in a not so good way. Warning! You will lose friends like that. No one wants to be with or talk to a person with a bad attitude. You must balance how to be confident within yourself but still respectful of others even if they have a different opinion.

I've always shown my creativity through the clothes that I wear. I have a unique style, mostly because it changes from day today based on how I feel. I typically do not like wearing colors that are too bright. I think that pastel colors are not very appealing on me. You may catch me wearing yellows and bright pinks once in a while. This normally happens when I need a quick outfit. I do LOVE SWEATERS! I have a lot of them. They are so easy to throw on. You can dress them up, down, or anything in between. When you find *that* article of clothing that you like, rock out with it. You'd be surprised that you can do the same with t-shirts. Just be creative and have fun with your clothes so that they will show the real you.

I started to become interested in makeup towards the end of my 7th grade year. By the 8th grade, I was all in. I had this idea in my mind that I would "glo up" before my first year of high school, so I started to watch "how to" videos.

SWNM MarQuita: Glo' up?

SWNM Niya: Mom.

SWNM MarQuita: Ok. Continue.

At the time, the major trend was eyebrows so I practiced that the most. I think I'm good at it now, but it did take a lot of practice. I would practice at random times just so I could get better and honestly, that's the key to makeup - practicing over and over again until you find what compliments you the most. At first, it can be hard to find what makeup will work best for your skin. Then again, you have a wonderful lady (aka Mom) that has already been through the process of what works and what does not. She can share techniques with you to make sure that you don't look crazy.

SWNM MarQuita: Right. Can't be out in these streets looking crazy!

Some girls may use makeup as a way to compensate for what they think they are lacking. Makeup should not be used for that because you should be confident in you, how you look without it, mostly because God made you beautiful already! Other girls may use cosmetics simply because they have feelings for someone. You should know that if a person really likes you, they will like you with or without makeup. I'm not saying that everyone uses makeup because they don't have confidence. I'm just saying that makeup should be used because it's fun, not because it's necessary.

Hair is a totally different story. Hair is so complicated that I still do not fully understand it. There are many hair types and even in those hair types there are different hair types. You can have 2A to 4C hair. I originally had type 4B hair, but then I got a texturizer, which made my hair less coarse. It was fun while it lasted. I have recently made the decision to go all natural again and it is very challenging. I know I'm not the only girl with hair problems. Your hair can be very thick and you can barely get a comb through it or it can be super thin. Hair problems are real! I know that if I haven't been taking good care of my hair, then I need to put it in a style that will protect it. Protective styles are amazing! There is such a variety of choices. Sometimes I'll get braids/individuals, and other times I'll get crochet braids. Both of these styles allow me to leave my hair alone so it hair can grow healthier; however, in some cases these protective styles can cause damage too. If you keep pulling on your hair, then it will start to become weak and might even break off or fall out in that area. I know a lot about this topic because I had a bald spot (it's growing back in) from too much tension caused by a braid. I'm okay with it but sometimes it's upsetting. I've learned how to deal with it, because I know how to pray and I have products that will grow the hair. It's certainly been a journey finding what works best for me.

After taking time to think and trying to be patient with the process of returning to my natural curl, I started thinking about the big chop. (For those who do not know what the big chop is, it is when you cut off the majority or in some cases all of your hair to get a fresh clean start). I had every kind of damage you could think of - chemical, heat and color. It was upsetting because I had stopped using heat and was moisturizing my hair faithfully but it was still dry. Most of all, my hair just wasn't growing. I felt deep down that I was going to have to do the big chop, but I didn't want to admit it. I watched videos on the process and how those who decided to go through with it felt about their decision. Well, during a trip to London, England, I finally just cut it off. In the beginning, I might have had about an inch or two of hair. People think that short hair is easier to take care of but they are soooooooo wrong. You have to do twist outs every night until you find a wash and go that works. For me, it took two months to find one but when I did, I was so happy. My curls looked nice and my hair was not dry. All in all, the big chop was the best thing that I could've done for my hair because now it is growing back pretty and healthy.

"But I discipline my body and keep it under control, lest after preaching to others I myself should be disqualified." **1 Corinthians 9:27**

My mom became very dedicated in working out and lifting weights. Her involvement really sparked my interest. Her involvement also changed the type of food that we eat. Bruh! I try eating more balanced foods and exercising, but it's hard because I can be the laziest person in the world (my mom wants me to stop saying this) and won't care about how unhealthy the food is.

SWNM MarQuita: I'll be so happy when you stop saying that you are lazy! You have power in the words that you speak. You know this. C'mon!

SWNM Niya: OK! OK!

My mom was there to guide me. She helped me when I needed the inspiration to be able to motivate myself. She also took me to the gym when I did not want to go and taught me how to use the machines and weights properly. I've grown to like it so I go often. My mom makes sure that I get a good workout in and that I focus in on the areas that I've selected. Working out is hard, but it becomes a lot easier for you when you have someone cheering you on.

The word "diet" is not used in our home. We prefer to use the terms "healthy living plan" or "lifestyle." When I decided that I wanted to live a healthier lifestyle, I had to learn how to cook more things so I could eat the healthier foods I wanted to try. Most people think that healthy foods are gross and they're right. (Just kidding!) I think anything can taste good if you have the right ingredients.

No matter how much you want to eat healthy, snacks and fried food will always be around. Some people will say that if you want to be fit you must always stay away from these foods. I understand their perspective, but I personally do not believe that at all. I think that it is okay to eat various kinds of food. You just can't eat them all of the time. If you learn how to balance your choices, you should be okay. My mom has always been there when she notices I've been eating more junk food to remind me to do better. Most times I don't notice it until she says something. She started to buy the 100 calorie snacks to prevent me from buying and eating the really bad ones. They're really not that bad. There are a lot of good food alternatives. I can't give you a list because I don't know many (LOL) but there are websites and books with tons of information at the push of a button. We all have to make good decisions to take care of the one body that we have.

Along with taking care of your external self, you have to learn how to make sure you're good on the inside. Have self respect. Don't let other people bring you down in your life journey. Be confident in what God gave you and love it. When you get to the place where you want to be, make sure you help others get to their place. Most likely, they're going to need the same things you needed to get there. Be a good person and lend a helping hand. In the end, what matters most is the person that you truly are, not the person that you may have spent all of this time trying to be. It's not always easy finding yourself with the worlds standards all around you but you can and you will. Take the time, and don't be too hard on yourself. Divas weren't born overnight!

This is how we do it:

- **(BD)** Divas set trends. If they choose to follow them, they'll still put their own spin on it. One of the ways we have fun is by being free to explore with different patterns, textures, and colors in regards to our clothing, hair, shoes, jewelry, etc. The motto in this house is, "Don't be boring." As long as it's appropriate (good fit, has you covered correctly), wear it! Don't allow other people's perspectives to deter your creativity. Some people will only wear black and white. Let them. You, on the other hand, wear all the colors of the rainbow should you feel so led to do. Just have the confidence to rock it!

- **(BD)** Be open to finding treasures in the most unpopular places. Some of my greatest pieces I have found on the rack in a thrift store. Match your lower cost pieces with good tailored pieces (that may be more expensive) and watch your wardrobe soar. Listen, cost does not always determine quality, and just because an item has a price tag on it does not mean that it has never been worn. If you know good quality designers and pieces, you can come out of consignment shops or thrift stores looking like you came out of a high-end boutique.

- **(BD)** So while we're on the subject of clothes, one size does NOT fit all! That is a lie straight from the lake. Don't fall for it. There is nothing worse than seeing an amazing piece destroyed because the purchaser refused to go up one size for the extra space needed, or they refused to leave the item in the store. Certain cuts demand larger sizes. Certain fabrics demand more room. It's okay to represent yourself in the best light possible.

- **(BD)** Know when to add and when to take away (makeup, weight, throwing out old things to make room for the new, etc.) In our home, we use each other as real mirrors. I am not afraid to tell Niya if something doesn't look good or if it's too much and I've charged her to do the same for me. We will say, "Hey there beautiful, you're eating too much junk food" or "That item doesn't fit as well now as it did before" or "That is way too much eyeshadow." Honesty is the foundation of healthy relationships. Having a good attitude towards constructive criticism secures that relationship. We also make it a point at least once every six months to go through our clothing, shoes and accessories to give the things away that we can or toss the things that are trash. Purging is a wonderful process.

- **(BD)** Embrace the old tried and true remedies. They work! Find what hair, makeup and cleansing products (natural or cosmetic) work for you. Be patient with the process. Save your money because you're going to need it! LOL! Listen to your support system as they attempt to keep you from falling out in tantrums every time something you buy doesn't do what you want it to do. Don't be discouraged. What you are experiencing is normal.

- **(BD)** Taking care of your body (eating right and exercising) is a must for a happy life. Don't wait until you get older, do it while you're young. If you have waited, today is a great day to start. You want to live a long, healthy life - mind, body, spirit and soul. We want that for you as well.

- **(BD)** I want to speak to parents who are dealing with children who are in that awkward phase of self-acceptance and self-esteem as their bodies are changing. We've all been there. We know how difficult it can be. Affirmations are a wonderful tool. Imagery/subliminal messages are wonderful tools as well. If your child is battling to see their beauty, you have to find the balance of showing it to them (through your words, your actions, and the time you spend) and allow them to find it for themselves. You can tell your child that they are the best thing since sliced bread, but if they do not believe it, it won't matter. Buy books, talk, link them up to empowerment/mentor groups. Buy, create and hang pretty signs in spaces that speak to what their souls need not what society provides. Your child may have an amazing relationship with one of your siblings or a close friend. Let them know if that person is a safe person to share with. Remember, sometimes our children will not talk to us about everything, especially if they feel that we've already discussed the topic over and over again.

Show your child how to laugh at pimples and bad hair days. Honor that although those things affect us, they are normal and they happen to everyone. Be there to dry every tear that you can. Never leave their hearts in the frail state that you find them. What works best for Niya and I is my vulnerability in being honest about my fears and insecurities with her. It gives Niya hope that if mommy has overcome her own struggles, laziness, and excuses to look how she looks now, to work how she works now, and to have what she has now, so can I. Most of all, teach your child that they cannot hide brokenness behind clothing, makeup and jewelry. The inner man will always shine through. Help them work through their emotions and settle your spirit to be in there for the long run. They'll thank you for it.

- **(LD)** Remember, hair is just hair. Don't be afraid to do what's best for it, even if it means cutting it all off. (Talk to your mom first!) Have confidence and rock your newfound hairdo. Love it and take care of it as best as you can. Low manipulation is best when try to get your hair strong and healthy again. You can do this!

- **(LD)** When it comes to makeup, don't rush to put on a full face. Start with a little here and there then work your way up. Please do not go out in public looking crazy! LOL! It takes patience and practice to do makeup well, so make sure you practice a lot. Try not to get frustrated when some things don't work out because you can just wipe it off and try again!

- **(LD)** LOL! I'm not sure what else to write here because I feel like I've explained everything in the chapter. **★Silence★** Yeah! That's about it.

Prayer

God, you made the heavens and the earth. At the end of every day of creation, you looked at the works of your hands and declared that it was good. We thank you for allowing us to be a part of those good things. Your word tells us that the very hairs on our heads are numbered. Wow!

You pay such close attention to your children. We've chosen the word "diva" in fun, but we really understand that the way that we chose to present ourselves is serious. It shows who you are to the world. We want to make you proud. Give us the grace to invest in the good creation that you've made us to be. Let us seek after ways to stay in the best shape possible both naturally and spiritually. Help us be able to receive and to give wise counsel and constructive criticism in love. Let us always see the beauty in ourselves and in others. Remove barriers that will keep us from uniting. Allow us the grace to accept our unique ways of thinking, dressing and living. Remove the sting that remains buried within us when others chose to degrade us and the collateral damage that it has caused to many generations. We want to be whole. We want to be free. Teach parents how to weather the challenges that come along with our children evolving. Give our children ears and hearts to receive the wisdom. You make everything beautiful in your time **(Ecclesiastes 3:11)** We thank you for that.

In Jesus name we pray, Amen.

Goal Diggers

Queen

I was sitting on the side of my bed one day when I clearly heard the following words from God's mouth to my ears: "A disciplined heart and a disciplined mind makes disciplined decisions." (The corners of my mouth immediately turned downward) What now, God? Discipline? We're here **AGAIN?** Ugh. I could try to come up with a deep philosophical reason to justify my initial reaction but that would be a waste of time. To the unlearned, discipline is cruel and unnecessary. As you mature you realize that discipline is a blessing.

SWNM Niya: A blessing?

SWNM MarQuita: Yes! A blessing!

SWNM Niya: How is getting in trouble a blessing?

SWNM MarQuita: There's more to discipline than punishment or correction Niya. Let me finish my thought please.

Discipline, or better yet *self-control* is a building block for great success. A wise builder knows to lay it at their foundation for the lessons it teaches are invaluable. Discipline gives us the ability to call our behaviors to the carpet. What behaviors? The "this is who I am, how I am, and what I do take it or leave it because it will never change" behaviors. Discipline removes excuses. It exposes impulsive and reactive natures. It uncovers our shortcomings or fears to simply try something different than what we've learned so that we can finally live according to God's design for our lives. **This** is a blessing. I've tried it so I know what I'm about to say to be true. You cannot reach any goal, whether it is a natural or a spiritual one, without discipline.

I was a self-motivated student in school. My mother really did not have to stay on top of me about completing my homework assignments. I would find programs to apply for in the summer to enhance my learning and broaden my perspective of all that life had to offer.

I liked getting A's and awards. I liked being able to go and come as she would allow because I was a successful student. That took discipline. The school I attended was not light on the volume of homework assignments. We had more than enough to keep us busy every night. Completion of assignments were a priority even on nights when we had to go to church. I sat in what was known as the "side room" many nights listening to Bible class while completing homework. You too? I know! The curriculum of the school I attended was so great that I was prepared to enter the wonderful world of academia high school through grad school. In each setting, I remembered the tools I acquired to remain disciplined. It wasn't easy, but it most certainly was worth it.

Sidebar: You want another example of something that was not easy to do? Something that took supernatural discipline to complete? Writing this book that you are reading! Do you know how hard it was to get my teenager interested in taking the time to write (and complete) a book? It was not on her list of things to do. The other activities that she was already involved in was her priority. Nothing more, nothing less.

SWNM Niya: *So true. I was not motivated to write this book at all let alone finish it. I was obedient though!*

SWNM MarQuita: *That you were!*

It was equally challenging to keep myself in line with the vision. This process is not for the faint at heart. Writing causes you to second guess yourself and your ability. You question everything. You want your gift to be received. You want the information to be relevant and helpful. Niya and I went through what seemed to be an endless cycle of starting and stopping. *Doing This Life Thing Together* would have never materialized had it not been for the power of discipline and a good ole' push from the Savior saying "Do what I told you to do NOW!"

SWNM Niya: *Mom. You started talking about one thing and went off about something totally different.*

SWNM MarQuita: *I did not go off on anything Simone. It's all relevant. Besides, that's what a sidebar is for. Now. Let me get back to discipline in education and learning. Thank you.*

SWNM Niya: *Stares and blinks eyes*

I've tried to teach my daughter to love learning. To become educated in a matter or a subject is to place yourself in a position to be sought after. When that occurs, the circle of learning never ends. As you pour into others, they pour back into you. What you learn can never be taken away. It took years of frustration but I finally realized that toddlers had the keys to the mysteries of life all figured out; especially when it comes to learning. The key lies within a question. A question that would open minds and hearts to experiences way past comfort zones and understanding.

To learn we cannot be afraid of the question "Why?" It's ok to ask Why do I feel the way that I feel? Why do I reply to certain stimuli the way that I do? Why do I believe that I belong to my family? Why do I believe that what my teachers are teaching me are facts? Why do I believe in Jesus? Why do I believe that I am blessed even in moments of confusion and despair? Why ask why? It's NEVER ending.

I've taught my daughter that many people will claim to have wisdom, but try them. You'll know if they are wise or not because wisdom will always produce good fruit. I've challenged her to never take anyone's word and make it gospel just because they said it. God has given us all a level of intelligence; therefore, we are compelled to operate in its fullness.

I don't know about you, but my dreams and goals feel so much bigger than anything that I could ever accomplish. My imagination is so vivid and so real where at times it has become a bit discouraging to my "reality." But what *is* my reality? Is it only what I see in my right now? Can't be. Something inside of me is pulling me towards so much greater. I have to remind myself of **Philippians 4:13,** "I can do all things through Him (Christ) who strengthens me." There is no limit. There is NO thing that I cannot do. ALL MEANS ALL. I couple that with **Ephesians 3:20,** "Now to Him (Christ) who is able to do far more abundantly than all (there's that word *all* again) that we ask or think, according to the power at work within us."

Hello honey! Did you read that? You have power in you. When you tap into that power (which is the Holy Spirit), it authorizes Christ to blow your mind! He will forever have the power, but He's not going to force anything on you. A properly installed electrical outlet will always have the power to work. You have to pay the bill to keep the electricity in your home. Paying your bill allows the utility supplier to give you authorization to use their product.

Some of the greatest enemies to reaching our goals is the management of our time, emotions, outside influences, and our space. Time management within itself is a great balancing act. At one point in my life, I had so many titles and held so many positions on so many different levels professionally and within my local assembly/church affiliated organization that I knew that it was God alone sustaining me and my daughter. I was, after all, a full-time mother. I could never afford to procrastinate. If I did, major balls would drop, many people would be affected, and I did not want to be responsible for that.

In wanting to save everything and everyone else, I neglected myself at times. Let me help you with this. I had to learn that busy bees are not always productive bees. You can be gifted, anointed, called and blessed with many gifts and talents. That's amazing. Pray and discern what gift, talent and ability God wants you to use at what appointed time and in what capacity. You cannot sing, preach, play the drums, usher, watch the kids, proofread an email, attend the cheerleading competition and bake cookies all at the same time. The first question I would ask someone attempting to do everything on their own is why? Why are you trying to do it all? May I submit something to you? If you are the only person that can do what you do (especially if you've called yourself a leader in any capacity) you have failed. I'm sorry, but it's true. (Actually, I'm not sorry. I repent. Wait, bow your heads so I can have a moment to get right.) You've failed!

One of the major goals of a leader should be the development of more leaders that ultimately supersede what they have accomplished. I want everyone that I have had the opportunity to teach, mentor, love on, instruct, or supervise to be **BETTER** than me. Period. If not, what were all of my tears, lessons and experiences for? Secondly, leaders must accept that there is only one of you. When approached with a task, I've learned (and am still learning) to ask if I can take a moment to pray and get back to the person. **PRIORITIZE** and weigh the pros and cons. Ask yourself, is this task aligned with God's plan for me? If no, gracefully bow out. If yes, seek wisdom on how to manage and incorporate it into your schedule.

Timelines and deadlines are our friends, better yet, accountability partners. They help to keep us on track. If I have a goal in mind with a set date and a guide for its completion, these two assist me with staying focused, especially when I need to weed out my own emotions (laziness, fear of failure, competing lists of things that are more important), outside influences (being everything for everyone and taking on everyone else's tasks for me but not completing what I am actually assigned to do) and space. Your mind is space, your heart is space, your home is your space. You have a duty to protect it at all cost.

Eject negative nouns (people, places and things). Keep your space clean and clear. You need to hear from God without having to sift through clutter. It may sound funny, but I am extremely picky on who I allow into my home. It is not that I think that my home is so grand that no one is worthy to cross the threshold. No! LOL! I just do not have many gatherings there. My home is the place where I can totally shut down, tune out, be as turned up, creative, prayerful, or peaceful as I want. My dreams and goals are written on my walls. God's word is written on my walls. Everyone cannot handle that and everyone cannot have access to that. Now, if you haven't been invited to my home, it doesn't mean that I have a problem with you. We all know Niya and I stay on the go! I've simply decided to keep socializing on the other side of the door. It works for me. Find what works for you.

Dreams and visions are snapshots from Heaven of our earthly assignments. If we keep this in mind, we in wisdom and with discipline are in a far better place to ensure that our plans align with God's plans. Again, we are taught to acknowledge Him in all of our ways. Ask Him, "Lord, is this dream or vision from you, or is that three piece and a biscuit with the side of red beans and rice speaking to me?"

SWNM Niya: *Oh. That would be good right about now.*

Ask "Lord, is this my will or my desire or is this you?" I fleece the Lord a lot. I ask alot of questions. I've never understood the "don't question God" thing. Well, if He's my father, my closest friend and everything else in between, why can't I have a conversation with Him? Did He not tell me to ask in order to receive? Did He not tell me if I lack wisdom to ask for it and He will freely give it to me? Yeah. I'm going to do that. I've been so in need of His direction and His answers that I've literally said that before I make this move or make this decision I need to see the Lord come down on a cloud wearing a purple robe with a cheeseburger in His hands for us to share.

SWNM Niya: *A cheeseburger sounds good too.*

SWNM MarQuita: *Hungry much?*

I'm not being disrespectful nor am I joking. This is how urgent His voice was in the matter. Now, I've never had this experience (as of yet) but I guess He said, "Let me answer this crazy child of mine clearly but in a less theatrical way so she can leave me alone." LOL! I know God laughs at me often. He does. You may be laughing at me too; but this is what I need you to understand. Every time I get to the point of asking for the purple cheeseburger experience, I receive clear confirmation. I receive help. Purple cheeseburger is like my distress cry. My distress hurts His heart so in these moments, as any good father would, God hears me, answers me and He saves the day. To go against God's plans is detrimental to everyone around you. His ways are not our ways; His thoughts are not our thoughts **(Isaiah 55:8)**. He knows the end from the beginning. We do not. What's more is if God has given you a dream, vision or a task, run with it for His word declares in **Philippians 1:6** "And I am sure of this, that He who began a good work in you will bring it to completion at the day of Jesus Christ." You do your part and let God take care of the rest.

Yes. I hear you. You're asking "So what's my part?" How do I prepare for the future when it is so uncertain? Do I live frivolously because none of us really know what the future holds? Do I squander away all of my time and money with no direction? God forbid. Let's discuss the parable Jesus taught in **Luke 19** of the Ten Minas (talent - a unit of weight/currency). It reads, "As they heard these things, he proceeded to tell a parable, because he was near Jerusalem, and because they supposed that the kingdom of God was to appear immediately. Calling ten of his servants, he gave the ten minas, and said to them, "Engage in business until I come." Here's a question for you? Are you taking care of business, the business for today and for the day when you are no longer here? Do you have savings accounts? IRAs? Life insurance policies? Do you own property? Yup! We're going there. Insert the financial soap box portion of the book.

When I was younger, the general public did not have access to the various ways of building material wealth like we do now. Financial freedom was not a topic taught within our church congregations. I was blessed to have a mother who always reminded my brother and I to, "Save something for later", "Put something to the side for a rainy day", or my favorite, "Don't spend all of your little money in one place." (Dukes, why is my money little? LOL! I digress.) My mother was trying to teach us the basic principles of saving. I always worked so I kept some change in my pocket. I wasn't introduced to debt until I entered into college. I'm not speaking of my college loans though some will argue that student loans are good debt and others will disagree. I'm not here to argue this point. What I do want to discuss is being met with tables upon tables of credit card companies my first day of undergrad right outside of the student union building. Every credit card company that you could imagine was awaiting to sign me up and give me trinkets for doing so. I did not pay attention to the interest rate. To be honest, I didn't know what that was; and it didn't matter. I had access to money and could get whatever I wanted NOW! No waiting! I took no thought to how I was going to pay the money back and definitely did not understand the power of the credit report/score. Needless to say, I messed up my credit before it had a chance to become established. I spent years repairing it. I'm still working to keep it straight (discipline).

I am passing this acquired knowledge to the offspring. I've always taught her to think before she makes a purchase but the conversations have increased as of late. I've taught her to decide if what she's about to buy will increase or decrease in its value. Is this item something that she'll actually use months from now or is it something that she can pass on to future generations? Yes. She needs to start thinking like this NOW so that it's second nature when the time comes for her to manage her own money. I'm teaching her the value of owning property, owning her car, owning licenses to her bodies of work. Own it. Prayerfully she learns from my experiences and will not have the same testimony as I.

SWNM Niya: *Mom, I'm only 15! LOL!*

SWNM MarQuita: *15 sounds like a good age to start building wealth.*

Parents, have you been honest with your children about money matters? In order to have an honest conversation with them, you have to have an honest conversation with yourself. What is your relationship with money? Is it positive or negative? What are your spending patterns? Are you an emotional/impulsive spender or a person who budgets effectively? Have you shown them a credit report and discussed how adverse reporting will affect their ability to reach their goals? Have you taught them in word and by your actions that it's okay to wait on purchasing things? Have you discussed the importance of savings? Have you discussed the blessing in paying offerings, tithes and donating to charity?

It is quite alright to desire wealth, to accumulate wealth and to spend that wealth. Money is not evil. The love of it is. When you'll do anything for a dollar, there is a problem. If when you get a dollar you spend a dollar, there is a problem. If you having nothing to show for all of the dollars God allowed you to make, there is a problem. I am in no way a financial expert, but I have experiences. Such as I have, give I thee.

As long as there's breath in our bodies we should plan for this life and, most importantly, the one after it. Discipline teaches the believer that the Messiah is returning and that we must be ready when that occurs. It is discipline that keeps us reading his Word, repenting daily, and submitting our fleshly desires to His will. It is discipline that teaches us to love our neighbors as ourselves and to forgive them as we would want Christ to forgive us. It is discipline that causes us to invest our time and money into church congregations and assemblies as they seek to reveal Jesus in our communities in a real and tangible way. Discipline wakes us up early in the morning to attend services and fellowship with other believers. Discipline makes us disciples. Disciples share the good news. We are literally living (planning) to live again. Everything we do while we live will be judged. With that in mind we pray to make good decisions to live eternally with Jesus in peace. This here IS the ultimate goal. Selah!

Princess

I have so many dreams and goals that thinking about them really makes my head spin. The thing is that most of my dreams and goals seem to be unrelated! It drives me crazy because I'm getting closer and closer to college and I have no idea of which dream I want to pursue. I can't get the thought out of my mind that I'm going to have to go out into the world on my own and that won't be easy. I have no clue of what I'll end up doing, but here is the list of things I've been thinking about: marine biology, movie production, massage therapy and maybe a singer but I wouldn't want to get my hopes up with that one. Do you get it now? Not one of my potential career choices complement the other!

Education is so important for my future. I don't want to admit it because I am not the biggest fan of school, but hey, to make my dreams reality, I gotta go to school. There's a nice amount of teens my age who would rather school not be a thing, and I can understand why.

At times, school feels like it's more about passing and a getting a certain grade than it is about learning and being able to apply what I've learned. We all just want to see those straight A's on our report cards. That can be easier said than done. Unfortunately, there are some people who will do anything to achieve that, even if it means cheating. **Deuteronomy 5:19** says, "You shall not steal." Cheating is basically stealing someone else's work.

I'm asking God to give me the desire to learn. This would make getting better grades easier. I must admit that I have taken advantage of opportunities given to me (which I should not do) when it comes to my education. There was a time in our country's history when my African American ancestors did not have access to higher learning. Slave masters did not want them to learn how to read or write. They could not go to certain schools. My ancestors were made to feel that they were less important than other races. I want to honor them by being successful. They worked very hard. They fought and died for millions of people they did not know, including me.

Finding a college that specializes in what I may want to do is a burden. It's kind of impossible when you don't know what you want to do! I would like to attend an HBCU (Historically Black College and University). Sometimes, I get really nervous about college because I'm not the best student all of the time. Don't get me wrong; I'm not failing anything. My mother views Cs as Fs so I'd never hear the end of it. I'm doing very well; I just don't get straight A's.

I also know that colleges look at more than just your grades. There are other qualifications that I will need to meet like community service, extracurricular activities, and scores for standardized tests. I'm sure that I'll learn a lot of important life lessons in college. I'll especially learn about time management. Time management is important because I have to be able to do everything I need to do without unnecessary stress. I'm aware that time management is not just a skill I need to have for college and my life after that. I need to learn it now. To be completely honest, I have terrible time management skills. I'll wait until the last minute to do anything. Let my mom tell ya! (It drives her crazy!) I even waited until the last minute to write this. She gave me a deadline and I missed it.

SWNM MarQuita: Confession is good for the soul.

I know I have to get much better managing my time or life may only get harder. To help me learn the value of time management, my mother has put the following things into place: I have to iron my clothes for school, church, or any activity the night before. My homework has to be done before I go to sleep. The chores I complete on Saturday has to be done by a certain time. I've learned that because of my hair type, I have to twist my hair if I want it to look nice in the morning. In my head, this seems like a lot because I'm lazy (pray for me) and I never want to do anything.

SWNM MarQuita: Here we go again with the lazy comment!

I pray that these practices will pay off in the end.

I need a quality education to have a quality career that pays WELL. A job is something you do for money temporarily. A career is something you do for the rest of your life. I need a career. I need one that will pay me the salary that I'll need to live how I want to live. My mom says that I am not cheap. She is not wrong.

SWNM MarQuita: *I know I'm not wrong. I have the receipts. TUH!*

I do like expensive things. I choose them even when I do not realize that they are expensive. My mother told me that my grandmother use to call her "poor little rich girl" because she had "expensive taste." She would naturally gravitate towards the high-end pieces in the stores all of the time. I guess I inherited that from her too! This is not a bad thing. I just have to be able to pay for what I want. That will take financial preparation. I'll have to be able to save money for sure.

It is important that I have money saved in case something pops up. For example, (looking at what my mom has had to do in our home) if a big appliance in my home breaks down, I need to have the money to replace it or get it fixed. I need to save money to be able to provide for my family and my future children. If they are anything like me then I will have my hands full with the cost of taking care of them. Hopefully I can survive! By saving money I have been able to buy my mom some **GREAT** presents. (Let me say that I did not want to write anything about buying my mom presents, but she made me do it. She even made the word great all caps.) I know it's not to brag, but to show you that if I can do it, you can do it too.

SWNM MarQuita: *That's exactly what it is. Young people need to know that it is possible to be on the giving side of the relationship with their parents. No bragging necessary. Teachable moment.*

I really love when I can show my mom appreciation for all of the things that she does for me. She loves presents, so I give them when I can. She also loves the handmade cards I make or the fact that she can come home to a cooked dinner and a clean home. Teenagers, learn your parents and make them happy. With the money I save, I am also able to buy things that my mom doesn't want to buy me. Usually the money that I save comes from birthdays, Christmas, summer jobs and little things I'll do on the side. If I know that there is an event coming up where I would have to spend money, I save until I need it. This way, I'm not rushing at the last minute trying to make some money. This skill will help in the future because I'll have to pay bills. Ugh. My mom has already started to talk to me about the importance of paying your bills on time and having good credit. The whole credit and interest thing is very confusing to me now, but I'm sure once I get older I'll have more questions and understand more.

I'm realizing that the plans that I have for myself may not be the plans God has for me. My career might be something that I've never even thought or dreamed of. Should that be the case, I have to stay strong and stay disciplined. I'll have to learn how to not doubt God when things don't go my way or don't go as planned.

I have to make sure that when I finally go out into the world by myself, I represent God. I know that there will be times when things may seem rough because life will make them that way, or there may be times that God will test my faith. I need to prove to Him that I will be His faithful servant. Listening to the testimonies of others, I know these things are easier said than done but they are doable.

My mom told me that when I was a child she gave me back to God. My life is His and I know that He will provide all that I need. Whatever God chooses for my life, I pray that He helps me to be satisfied with it because I know He always has my best interest at heart. In the end, I want to make it into heaven! I know I can only do this by living a holy life and by staying devoted to God. I will have to make sacrifices because my way isn't always the right way. I'm willing to make them if I know His way will lead me to heaven to be with Him.

This is how we do it:

- **(Q)** The writing is on the wall.   No, really it is. In the kitchen, in Niya's room and in the hallway. **Habakkuk 2:2** declares, "And the Lord answered me: 'Write the vision; make it plain on tablets, so he may run who reads it.'" Creating a clear and tangible plan saves time. It keeps you task-centered, as it reminds you of the goals you have set and it holds you accountable. This plan should include who is responsible for what part of the plan and should set timelines for completion. Consider this plan a living document. A living document is a document that can be continually changed and edited. When the dream, the goal and vision is of God it will not change. The road to completion however, may. Do not be afraid to update the methods you use to get to the end result.

- **(Q)** Prayer- what else can I say about prayer? It is essential before you make any moves. Period.

- **(Q)** Accountability partners.   How many of us have them? We all need them. Accountability partners hold your feet to the fire. They are the individuals you can trust with your God plan. They are the individuals you can trust to tell you the truth about how you are working or mishandling the God plan. Do not make the mistake in believing that your friends or family (no matter how wonderful they may be) are automatically accountability partners. Certain friends have certain purposes. If you are not careful, you will destroy great relationships giving unqualified people a voice to speak in areas of your life that they should not be privy to.

You may also miss out on a blessing by not allowing someone to give you words of life because you are so familiar with them that you can't see past the friendship. Revisit the bullet point above and pray about who your accountability partners should be. My daughter and I are each other's accountability partners with certain things. Healthy eating, wearing our braces, wrapping our hair are a few examples. Some things are simply not appropriate for her to know or handle at her age, and because our dynamic is still in the "I have the authority" phase. Some things she probably does not want me to know, so I cannot be the accountability partner. However, if I sniff it, I'm talking about it. Just call me super sleuth! LOL! We are mother and daughter, yet we are sisters in Christ. Whomever is the spiritual one in the moment has to be in a place to restore the other in meekness. Age and familial relationship means nothing when the restoration of a soul is a necessity.

- **(Q)** Nagging.   When all of the intelligent, super deep, emotionally supportive stuff seems to go in one ear and out of the other with your teenager- NAG THEM TO DEATH to complete their goals! It works. Scouts honor!

- **(Q)** Savings and budgets.   I started saving for Niya from birth (that's my mommy responsibility), but I did not always budget. There's a huge difference between the two. Ultimately, you should NEVER touch your savings until it reaches the determined time you've set for it. For example, you may have a vacation savings account or a Christmas savings account. These accounts have a specific purpose with a specified date. Saving for college, a wedding, or to buy a house requires a more detailed, long term savings plan which is more intense. I was saving without budgeting the money I had left to spend on my essentials and recreation. Because of this, I had to dip into my savings more than I should have, depleting it multiple times until I got it right.

Not wanting Niya to inherit this negative behavior, I decided to actually give her financial responsibility at a young age. To teach her how to save once she became a teenager, I opened an account with a company that would give her a card that she could use as a credit or debit card. Instead of giving her cash for her allowance, the amount (currently one dollar for every year of life plus 3) automatically loads on her card every week. From that account, one dollar automatically debits from her card to a savings account that she *CANNOT* touch. She's paying herself first. She can use her allowance as she pleases.

Once it's gone, it's gone. The thought behind this process is that I'm teaching Niya financial responsibility. I am also trying to rip the awe out of credit cards. At this point, she knows how it feels for money to hit an account at the same time every week. She knows what it feels like to swipe a card. Hopefully it works.

I have discussed the necessity of building credit and have asked her to allow me to walk through the process when she does decide to get a credit card. I know a little something now. One good card with a low interest rate is all that she needs. Niya and I have also split the bill for some of the larger ticketed items that she wanted. I need her to understand that money most certainly does not grow on trees.

By making her invest, I've saved a lot. How? Well, most of the time she changed her mind when her money became a part of the equation. There have also been times when Niya did not change her mind so I completely paid for the item because she was willing to invest in it. Rebuilding credit is difficult but not impossible. Start with prayer. Ask God to show you how to create and remain faithful to a plan. Stay out of the mall or offline. No one can fix this but you. Do your research if you use a credit repair company. If you find them reputable stick to the plan. Be patient as you watch the debt you owe decrease and your credit score increase. Hey, you have nowhere to go but up!!!

- **(P)** Stay focused. If you're worried about what everyone else is doing, you'll never complete what you need to get done. After all you're not living their life, so focus on bettering your own and being able to supply your own needs. Of course, if you have the support of your family, a boyfriend/husband, then you can lean on them a little but still I don't think it's good for people to depend on other people for everything.

- **(P)** When it comes to college, find a path you want to pursue, pray about it and stick to it. Maybe you can get a small job so you can begin to save money (depending on how old you are). This money could help with the expense of college tuition or help you to get a car to get around in while you're there. It can really help with any of your expenses. My mom taught me that. Here's another little tip: Try not to spend all of your money on things that you can get your mom to buy you like food and games. I will literally spend all of my mom's money on these two if she would let me. Not a good thing.

SWNM MarQuita: Oh, really!!! I see. I'll have a no or two in my pocket next time.

- **(P)** Make sure you honor and represent the people who did/do so much to make sure you'll have not only the things you need, but want. You honor them by getting a good education and good grades. It's what they fought for you to have so you can't just let them down by being lazy. That's easier said than done, I know, but it's the truth.

Prayer

Lord your word teaches in **Proverbs 14:12**, "There is a way that seems right to a man, but its end is the way to death." You are life, and since that life resides within we choose to live and not die. We pray you help us to discipline our ways, our thoughts, and our actions so that we may please you and become who you've designed us to be. When we allow you to order our steps, God, they become good. We prosper when we align ourselves with your plans. We must admit that "nevertheless" places us at your feet in total surrender, a place we may not always want to be, although it really is the only place to be. We repent and ask you to forgive all of the times we've gone astray from the clear safe path. We repent for the times we caused ourselves needless pain. We pray you forgive us for those moments where we ignored your voice chasing after those things that brought us to the way of death. As a good father, we know you forgive and receive us. We know that you will teach us the ways of life and that you will delight in us as we trust you more. Our lives, our dreams, our goals and our plans are safe in your care. We reject negativity. We reject failure. We are who you say that we are. You called us blessed. We are the righteousness of God. We are Abraham's seed. We are blessed and it cannot be reversed. We are the head and not the tail, above only and not beneath. We are the lender and not the borrower. We will possess land. We will evolve in your might and power to be a testimony of your great strength. How powerful you are, oh God, to take dirt and make something beautiful out of it. We are beautifully designed, an array of your splendor. We just want to please you. Please grace us with the discipline to do so.

In Jesus name we pray. Amen.

Love. Yeah. Still trying to figure this out.

Sensei

Can I be honest here for a moment? This is probably the second hardest chapter for me to write (parts of chapter two being the first). I've written and erased it so many times simply because I didn't know where to start (or end). Love can be a very sensitive subject, especially for females. It appears that we desire to share and experience love in a way that is more heightened than our male counterparts.

Here's the reason. From the moment a female child is born, she is inundated with the necessity of reaching her happily ever after. It starts with the receiving blankets covered with hearts and the word *love* beautifully scripted in the same font found on the most elegant wedding invitations. It progresses to the classic princess cartoons where the damsel in distress is rescued by a man who falls so deeply in love with her that he will risk it all. It trickles on down into the television shows that our children watch that glorify what we describe as "puppy love." It is found in the subliminal messages attached to the music that we hear until it is a part of the very fiber of our being.

We do our best to present ourselves as women of worth. We have our lip gloss, hairdos and beat faces down to a science. We buy into the fashion fads and spend thousands of dollars on things to adorn our outward appearances. We work hard. We go to school and earn degrees or pick up a trade in preparation for the great day a-comin', the one before the rapture. The one waaaaaayyyyy before the rapture. The day when the man of our dreams will finally "find us" and take our hands in marriage.

It's exciting and it's wonderful - except for when it isn't. Time has granted me the opportunity to think long and hard about marriage. Of course, my perspective on the reasons why I want to marry, what I believe my place in a marriage should be and what I desire to experience within a marriage has completely changed from my young adult years. Should love knock on my door at this very moment... (Hold on, I think I hear someone at the door. No, no one? It was just my imagination? Oh ok. I'm back) ...am I ready? Am I capable of meeting all of the needs for one man for the rest of our lives together? Is there a man somewhere in this great big world designed specifically for me? Lord knows he has to be designed specifically for me. Down through the years, I've been told to, "Wait on the Lord", "He's on his way", "God has someone special for you", "God has not forgotten about you", and "Be not weary in well doing." Must I continue?

Scripture after scripture. Cliché after cliché. I've heard them all. 6am prayer circles, single ministry workshops, relationship books. I've been there, done that, and **I'M OVER IT!** (You gasp? It's ok. I'll give you a minute to catch your breath). The scriptures are great, really they are. The encouragement was needed and appreciated. God's word is appropriate in every situation, so although His word is hidden in my heart that I might not sin against Him, life has taught me that in the real late, crazy and lonely moments, quoting the scripture doesn't always soothe the broken heart. Maybe it has for you. Maybe you've never been lonely. Maybe you've been married from the moment it became legal for you to marry. That's not my testimony.

It is a basic human need to relate and to be intimately attached to others. I know what love is and what it is supposed to be Biblically. I've heard it all my life. His Word declares it to be so in 1 John 4:8 "...God is love."

I have questioned why LOVE, who is MY father, would not allow this one true "human" love to manifest himself and find me. I've gone through the complete gamut of emotions and the list of questions that accompany them: "What's wrong with me?" "Am I too much?" "Am I not enough?" "Am I intimidating?" "Am I too strong?"

True story: I was once told by a group of older women in church that I had accomplished too much on my own and that was the reason why I had not been found. Men want women that they can be superheroes for, and I, I had the "S" on my own chest. Little did they know that it wasn't there by choice. Hear me and hear me good. I am, in no way, a part of the "I don't need no man" movement. My education, success and forward mobility was necessary. I do not apologize for it. At the same time, I am tired of having to make major life decisions alone. I'm tired of being solely responsible for the repairs to the house, taking out the trash, taking the car for tune-ups and improvements, and shoveling the car out during snowstorms.

SWNM Niya: Hey, I help with that too!

SWNM MarQuita: You do help me shovel out the car.

I'm tired of having to pay for ALL of the bills in my home. Sir, you want to fly in to save the day, here's your landing strip, but make sure you're built for it.

The man that marries me receives an automatic 2-piece. I have a child who has always been my priority. I have to believe (here's the purple cheeseburger thing) that this man will love my child as if she was the fruit of his looms (I mean loins).

SWNM Niya: What does that mean?

SWNM MarQuita: This is a conversation for another time. ★Thinks about it and continues★ All it really means is...

SWNM Niya: Nope. It's alright. Move on.

I have to believe that there will be no issues with their level of love and respect for one another as it relates to who they are in my life. I must believe that his decisions are Godly decisions because those decisions not only affect me, they affect her. I must believe that his plans for our family, naturally and spiritually, will lead us down God's paths for us. I want to be able to crawl in his arms and breathe, relinquishing all fear, knowing that we are safe in every way imaginable because who's got this thing? My husband does. Who has him? God does. With that in place, we're okay. If I cannot trust this, then what shall I say to these things? Negative roger. It's a no go. I'll pass. It's just that serious for me. I've had to mature to this place of revelation. It is quite easy to settle when what you desire does not manifest itself in the time that you believe that it should. The Bible says that hope deferred makes the heart sick, but a desire fulfilled is a tree of life **(Proverbs 13:12)**. *Cue the violins** Sweet soon and coming Savior, where's my tree? I like trees too! I like tall strong trees with great limbs. He needs to be rooted and grounded. His leaves cannot wither Lord and...

SWNM Niya: *Can you stop with all of this extraness?*

SWNM MarQuita: *What? Am I going off on a tangent here? I am?*

Anywho, in an attempt to "lower my standards a bit," another suggestion given to me by older women in their "how to catch a man moments," I found myself considering and in some instances actually entertaining (by entertaining I mean only talking to not having sex with) almost every "type" of man but the "right one" (obviously). Let's see. Well there was the pastor, the preacher, the musician, the singer, the preacher/musician/singer combo, the super deep/super saved where even when he was joking, he spoke in fake tongues using every bit of church jargon known to man, screaming, "YAAASSS" and using the word "girl" in a sentence more than me guy.

There was the totally unsaved thug, the half thug/half believer, the church player, the "I just want to be seen in public with you cause you are a good look for me", the "I don't know how to relate to anyone behind closed doors" guy, the "I'm a public success but private mess" guy, The "I want you for a notch on my belt" guy, the "If you don't give me what I want I'll try to destroy your name" guy, the "I love you but I'm not ready" guy, the older guy, the younger guy, the guy my age, the great guy that just wasn't great for me (most do NOT fall in this category), the friend who pronounced his undying love for me who should have kept that all to himself, the spoiled brat, the think he's a player but I'm actually ten steps ahead of him guy...

Get the point? It's so exhausting. I'm ready for the "He is the breath that I need to breathe even when it stinks, I don't mind giving him kids (and we all know my motto is "One per customer"), cooking his dinner, washing his clothes, even when you make me mad you're worth every tear, you're stuck with me for life, I can honor you because you fear, serve and honor God, you love our family and will protect us, you are consistent in who you are and your desire to grow with me, you work hard, save and invest for our future, you love and understand my strand of crazy, you want to travel and explore as much as I do" guy. Anything else is not worth it. Our destiny is too important, the anointing that God has on our lives is too important, peace is too important for foolishness.

I've tried to be the best walking example for my daughter, although I know at times I've failed. I've been extremely intentional in how I handle dating. Put one finger in the sky. That's how many men in her 15 years of life that my daughter can ever acknowledge as "mom's man." There was one other man that she knew I had real interest in. I did not need her experiencing heartbreak after heartbreak, disconnection after disconnection whenever I disassociated myself from someone that I introduced into her life.

There's a great reason for that. She is not to be played with. It appears that *some* of the men that I've encountered (I say some as I dare not categorize all men based on the subset found in my experiences) view love as a sport. It's a game. The ways of the world have made it acceptable for commitment to a wife to be "optional." A man will relentlessly hunt a woman down, date, impregnate and live with her and still not give her his last name in holy matrimony which really is the greatest honor that he can initially give to her.

Unfortunately, some women have made it so easy for men to disregard us in this way. We show men everything, we give men everything, and we trust everything. We've also adapted this "Imma get mine" mentality. Some women really could not care less about commitment. I've been there a time or two myself.

Beloved, for a brief moment in my life, I settled into living with a man that I was not married to. I cooked for him, washed his clothes, and cleaned his home. I basically played a role because I wanted the experience that I did not have growing up. What I failed to realize (although I was warned against it) was that the only experience I gained was the pain of what not to do.

There was no reason for this man to marry me. He received everything he needed from me without making any sacrifice or taking on any responsibility for me. His words and empty promises were just that - words and empty promises. Caring and doing, sacrificing and living for someone means nothing when they are not ready or not considering you as their mate. Having sex with a man won't keep a man faithful. Not having sex with a man may intrigue him and make you a conquest or challenge. He'll remain interested until he succeeds in his conquest or because he likes what you gave him. Either way, interest is not commitment. He'll place his flag on your belly as if to say "so-and-so" has been here and move on. Think I'm wrong? Change his access to you. Change your thoughts about yourself. Ask some questions about your future together. Come back to this chapter and reread it. What say ye?

Only the power of God (if he allows it to operate) will keep a man loyal to you in a covenant relationship. Until your covenant man comes, keep your goodness and mercy to yourself! LOL! Goodness and mercy are the terms I use with my daughter and other young women when I speak about their most precious and private areas. The terminology was actually birthed in the middle of a church service where a young lady that I did not know started raising her dress up above her head. I quickly pulled it down and said, "Oh no, don't ever show the world your goodness and mercy." "Goodness and mercy?" she asked. I replied "Yes, your goodness and mercy." I touched my chest. She mimicked where my hand landed on herself, looked down and asked again "Goodness?" I smiled at her and said, "You'll understand it by and by. No one should touch it or see it until it's time." She smiled at me and ran away.

I went to her mother after the service was over and explained our conversation. I've been using this ever since. If only I had taken my own advice! Am I helping somebody? I hope that I am. We all need confidants, people to look up to, people we can listen and learn from, a mentor or two. Our life experiences may be different, but that's what makes them powerful.

Let me offer you a piece of advice. Wait. Do not allow yourself to get caught up on enticing words and temporary feelings. You have to allow a man to prove himself to God first and then to you. If you're not careful, you'll be entertaining wolves in sheep's clothing, going out of your mind, finding yourself on the side of the road with ashy knees, a bad perm, trying to use twizzlers for rollers. Calm your fears, calm your anxiety, and calm your mind from racing. What's for you is for you. He's not going anywhere unless he's supposed to. If that is the case, rejoice! You'll learn in time that God was protecting you from something. Hey, I'm only telling you the truth because I care. I really do. Learn from me please.

It's great if you desire a mate, however, getting married just to fit everyone else's thoughts of what should happen in your life is a mistake of epic proportions! People settle into marriages and are unhappy because they did not pray and ask God to reveal the truth about themselves first and the person they are considering to marry. I know many a marriage that should have never happened. God did not join them - the preacher's words did. You know of these marriages too. The individuals got married because they wanted to have sex, they already had sex and were pregnant, everyone has been matching them up since birth, they needed to prove a pointless point because people are now questioning their sexuality, they're getting old...you know what I'm talking about! Now they are extremely depressed, mentally, emotionally and physically abused, unsatisfied, cheating and committing adultery, are addicted to pornography, bitter and unforgiving. If the time is not right, I don't want it. I don't want it far more than I do.

Are we doing a disservice to our children by religiously teaching them that if they act a certain way, and do certain things that one day someone will love them enough to marry them? Are we setting our children up for a wave of unnecessary emotions of failure, low self-esteem, and the like if they are not "found"? Could it be that not all are supposed to marry? Has it crossed your mind that God gives peace and contentment to those who aren't and that we should not look at them as if they are missing something or shun them as if they have leprosy? Mom and dad, have you given any thought as to how will you support your child if this is their lot? Deep, right? I've been praying for Niya's husband from day one.

SWNM Niya: *Yes Gawd!*

SWNM MarQuita: *Yes Gawd?*

SWNM Niya: **Giggles**

I've prayed and still pray that he is a man after God's heart for her. I pray he loves her as Christ loved the church and that He is willing to give his life (physically, emotionally, financially, spiritually) for her. I pray she marries a man who will never stifle her gifts, purpose and identity because of jealousy, insecurity, or strife. He needs to be her greatest cheerleader. (Now, it's going to be hard for him to out cheer me, but if he's faithful to the cause his efforts will not go unrewarded) Lolol! I pray that she marries a man that absolutely loves, respects and honors his mother and father. I pray that the family she marries into loves her and all future grandchildren unconditionally. I pray for a man who is intelligent and educated with not only dreams and goals, but a plan and a proven track record of success. A man who cares about his community and people. I pray that my daughter and her husband keep Christ first and that they are wise enough to keep outsiders out of their relationship. I pray that I will mind my business and let her work through her marriage giving words of wisdom when asked. I pray they are each other's best friend. I pray for their communication. I pray for their sex life. I pray for their health and the health of my future grandchildren. I pray that this man actually exists, and that my daughter can identify him when he comes and can welcome him honorably. I pray that if it is not God's will that we (yes, we) are okay with it, for she is still beautiful, complete and whole.

I've written a bit about love as it relates to men and women romantically, but romance is not the only type of relationship that is important. Friendships are essential. Love may start with our families, but it spreads itself abroad. Think about it this way, Jesus loved us so much that He died not only for the Jews (the chosen people, HIS people) but also the Gentiles (the rest of us). There are scriptures that speak to the strength of friendship. Let's explore a few of these for a moment.

John 15:13 reads, "Greater love has no one than this, that someone lay down his life for his friends." Friend. Not grandmother, not parent or child, not boo-thang, but a friend who really is a person you can choose or choose not to relate with. In **John 15:15** Jesus declared, "No longer do I call you servants, for the servant does not know what his master is doing, but I have called you friends, for all that I have heard from my Father I have made known to you." Wow!

The Father could make us all serve Him out of fear and exert His power whenever and however He decides to, but He does not. The maker of this universe calls us friends. **James 2:23** reads, "Abraham believed God, and it was counted to him as righteousness" and he was called a friend of God. The word *called* stands out so much for me in this moment that I really want to scream! Called, as in identified as, defined as, respected as. In order for someone to identify or define you as someone meaningful in their lives, you've either had to do something to earn their respect, or you've done something to keep their respect. Sometimes it's as simple as how you've handled their gift of friendship that was freely given to you.

I'd like to believe that Abraham's belief (faith) caused God to respect him. That respect was counted as righteousness (the good that was done) and because of that, Abraham became identified as God's friend - so much of a friend that God could tell Abraham to get up, leave all that you know, and I'll show you where you're going. So much of a friend that Abraham obeyed. Theirs was a friendship where God would send a messenger telling him that he was going to give him a son by the wife that he loved during his old age. A friend so much so that God would spare that same son in the moment that Abraham was going to offer his life as a sacrifice, warn him to get out of Sodom and Gomorrah before He destroyed it, and so forth and so on.

Oh! Chill bumps! The testament of friendship! Once you are called a friend and you accept the calling, you are protected, you are provided for, and you are involved in the process every step of the way. I want to ask Abraham, "Father A, how are you with all of your many sons? Good? Good. Any of them available? I'm asking for a friend. No? Okay listen. I have a question for you. What does it feel like to be a friend of **GOD**?"

SWNM Niya: *SINGS* "...He calls me friend."

Could you imagine asking Elijah what was going through his mind when God sent a chariot of fire to come and pick him up? We get hype when our friends pick us up for the movies so we don't have to drive and pay for parking! A chariot of fire from heaven though? WOW! There are so many mind-blowing examples of relationships with God in the Bible that...wait...wait. ***Heart beat racing*** These stories are amazing. Amazingly amazing.

Wanna know what's more amazing? The realization that **I AM A FRIEND OF GOD TOO!** He calls me friend not because of what

I deserve. It's really not based off of what I could give Him either. It's because I accepted the love He freely gave to me. **Romans 5:8** reads, "But God shows His love for us in that while we were still sinners, Christ died for us." God showed His love so much that He died while we were in a place of rejecting him, were unappreciative and had no interest in the sacrifice that He made. He died for us, planning for our redemption while we remained clueless that we ever needed it. He endured all of that with the hashtag #IDidItForMyFriends.

Now that you're friends, have you ever thought of what it actually requires to keep your friendship with God intact? How about your friendships with other human beings? In my opinion, the requirements are the same. It takes a mutual respect and a willingness to sacrifice. (We kind of touched on these already. Not many of us are required to die for someone, but we will have to sacrifice precious moments of our lives for others).

I believe friends must have things in common. You have to share some of the same interests and at least build up the tolerance for the few differences that you will definitely have. You have to enjoy each other's company, conversation, and space. Friendships require trust. Both parties must trust that their friend will always operate in integrity in their regard. Both parties must be fully persuaded that their friend will always fight for them and their honor. If you cannot trust that a person will support you (in your not-so-great times more than your good), why are they *called* your friend?

Psalm 55:12-14 "For it is not an enemy who taunts me, then I could bear it; it is not an adversary who deals insolently (rude and arrogant with disrespect) with me, then I could hide from him. But it is you, a man, my equal, my companion, my familiar friend. We used to take sweet counsel together, within God's house we walked in the throng." In other words, IT WAS MY HOMIE, MY HITTA, MY JAWN!!! It was the girl I told all of my secrets to. The youth group that I went to the movies with. The group I sat at the lunch table with every day. The women in the church that prayed with me and called me sister. Yup, them! Hurtful? Yes. The end of the world? Not a chance.

Friendships demand a certain level of accountability. I am accountable to be present, to tell you the truth even when it hurts, and to be strong when you're weak. I am accountable to be your friend and not your fan. Here's what I mean. A fan is interested in you based off of who you appear to be or what you claim to do. A friend knows you inside and out. A fan will blow up your head. Fans will applaud your moves even when they are dangerous, underhanded and totally contrary to God's will for your life. Their concern is simply staying connected for whatever it is that they can get from you (the old fishes and loaves experience). They practice selective loyalty. They'll allow you to be a loose cannon without pulling you back in.

Friends will tell you, "Yo, you are messing up big time." A friend will pull your coat tail. Friends will risk it all for you to be the good person that they chose to befriend. I've learned that friendships do not die because someone told the truth about a situation. Friendships die when people show the truth of their character and their connection. I'll tell you something else. I know that this is not true in all cases, but whenever I hear someone refer to another as "friend and brother" (or the female equivalent of this statement), I start looking for the entrance site of the knife they have in the person's back. No loyalty. Convenient relationships. We should do better.

I try to teach Niya that she is to always be who she claims to be to whomever she's made the claim to. She should expect people to do the same in her regard. I share with her that the truth behind a relationship will remain hidden but for so long so love; love freely, but be wise. Laugh and laugh often, but be wise. Share and share often, but be wise. It's easy to become so comfortable with people that you think you will be the exception to the rule in relation to how they mishandle people, until you're not. The Bible warns us about watching the company we keep. They are a reflection of who we are.

Lastly, friendships challenge you to grow. **Proverbs 27:17** "Iron sharpens iron, and one man sharpens another." I am inspired, challenged, uplifted and refocused whenever I am around my friends. They are a great group of people making moves to be better and to leave a mark on this world. If you find yourself always being the most intelligent, the most influential, and the most accomplished person in all of your circles, there is a problem, and that problem lies within you. There will always be someone who will know more than you, have experienced more than you, may even have greater influence in a certain area or place then you. Do you shun them? No. Become jealous? Absolutely not. You, with pure and sincere intentions, get to know them and welcome the lessons you'll learn from simply being around them. Hey, you may develop a friendship that you'll both enjoy.

We can always count on our heavenly Father to hold up His end of the friendship contract. Can He count on us to hold up ours? There's been so many times where Christ should have said to me, "I'm not your friend no more!" Yet, He's never spoken those words. He's forever faithful. That closer than a brother love is real **(Proverbs 18:24).**

The good thing is there are those ordained by God to walk through life with you. Those who will not waiver in their love for you. Those who will support you when you are batting one hundred, and tell you when you need some work on your swing. A friend loves and celebrates you with no strings attached. Friends are those people that you can disagree with, maybe even argue with and know that when you hang up or part ways nothing has changed. Here's a little something about MarQuita: I don't agree with myself all of the time, so why would I expect someone else too? That is totally unrealistic.

Distance is not a determining factor when it comes to the value of a friendship. I have friends that I speak to maybe once or twice a year, however; when we speak or meet up, it's as if we've never parted. I have people who I use to see all the time that prayed for my demise with the same tongue they called me "sis" with. The reason, season, or lifetime saying is true. Your life journey will certainly show you the stops that each person must get off.

It is my sincere endeavor to be that person that those that I love can depend on. This is who I am also teaching my daughter to be. It starts at home with the little things. If she says she's going to do something for me, I hold her to it. If she tells someone else that she is going to do something for them, I hold her to it. If she gives her word, I hold her to it. It's not okay to be flaky. I've also tried to teach her to be open to friendships with the most unexpected people. So often, we ignore the gifts of friendships that God has sent to us because we don't like the packaging. We'd rather wait for an opportunity to be with the most popular people or who we may consider the movers and the shakers. Be clear, the movers and the shakers will move right along without you and shake all memories of your friendship out of their mind when they are good and ready to. That quiet young lady or young man over there in the corner though, they may be lifers. Give them a chance.

One of the greatest secrets to all successful relationships is found in forgiveness. I began touching on this a little in Chapter 2. There is no perfect human. Sing it with me "No not one, no not one." Yes. Some of us have an extra petty gene that is not of God. In the end, it doesn't matter who is right and who is wrong. It matters that you forgive. The Bible is so specific on how this is to occur.

Have you ever had an argument or disagreement with someone where you knew that they only apologized to either: 1. Silence you because they are tired of arguing with you, 2. Silence you because they know it would make you more upset that they have silenced you, or 3. So that they could have the ability to say they apologized first, even though they really do not want to apologize at all? I've found myself in every situation! I've found myself forgiving people who never apologized. Those who will never admit that they were wrong. Those who rally people together in an attempt to destroy my influence, character and light. Forgiving those who are self-righteous to the point where they are reprobate. Those who said all of the things they needed to say to get what they wanted from me. Those who told me to forgive, but lack the ability to do it themselves.

I've found myself not wanting to accept an apology because I felt that the person should have known better. I equated their actions to a lack of love for me. I've lost patience with people who with words apologized, but their actions remained the same. "You get one time to…" That's normally my motto. When I forgive you and then you do it again, it's a wrap. I'm not saying it's right. It is true. Pray for me. I'm trying.

Forgiveness is so powerful that we've been given a formula to help us to administer it. **Ephesians 4:32** reads, "Be kind to one another, tenderhearted, forgiving one another, as God in Christ forgave you." In order to forgive someone, we must first be kind (benevolent, compassionate). Then we must be tenderhearted (gentle, meek). Tis the opposite of my natural response, which would be to first figure out what angle of this person's face I'll strike with as much force as possible. Kind and tenderhearted are terms that cause me to have to consider myself, forgetting myself before I place any type of judgment on someone else. It's about choosing someone else first and dying to my need and desire to be right, to be heard, to be vindicated, even when the person may (in my opinion) deserve every bit of pain that could come their way.

Stop it! Don't act like you do not think in this manner also. You, like me, have thought and justified it incorrectly with scripture. "You know the Bible says touch not my anointed and do my prophet no harm." Foolishness! Love covers a multitude of sin. Love forgave before the sin was committed. Knowing it was going to happen, He still chose us. God by manifesting Himself in flesh as His son Jesus showed us forgiveness. Isn't He amazing?!!

Forgiveness is a freeing agent. I love the story of the woman and the alabaster box in **Luke 7:36–50**. Let's read it together. "One of the Pharisees asked him to eat with him, and he went into the Pharisee's house and reclined at table. And behold a woman of the city, who was a sinner, when she learned that he was reclining at a table in the

Pharisee's house, brought an alabaster flask of ointment, and standing behind him at his feet, weeping, she began to wet his feet with her tears and wiped them with the hair of her head and kissed his feet and anointed them with the ointment. Now when the Pharisee who had invited him saw this, he said to himself, "If this man were a prophet, he would have known who and what sort of woman this is who is touching him, for she is a sinner." And Jesus answering said to him, "Simon, I have something to say to you." And he answered, "Say it, Teacher." "A certain moneylender had two debtors. One owed five hundred denarii, and the other fifty. When they could not pay, he cancelled the debt of both. Now which of them will love him more?" Simon answered, "The one, I suppose, for whom he cancelled the larger debt." And he said to him, "You have judged rightly." Then turning toward the woman, he said to Simon, "Do you see this woman? I entered your house; you gave me no water for my feet, but she has wet my feet with her tears and wiped them with her hair. You gave me no kiss, but from the time I came in she has not ceased to kiss my feet. You did not anoint my head with oil, but she has anointed my feet with ointment. Therefore I tell you, her sins, which are many, are forgiven—for she loved much. But he who is forgiven little, loves little." And he said to her, "Your sins are forgiven." Then those who were at table with him began to say among themselves, "Who is this, who even forgives sins?" And he said to the woman, "Your faith has saved you; go in peace."

Here it is: Her sins, which are many, are forgiven, for she **loved** much. But he who is forgiven little, loves little. This woman simply accepted the call to friendship, which ultimately, is the call to love. You can't give what you have not received. I look at my scars and I say "thank you Jesus" because I am this Luke 7 woman who was forgiven of much. I am this woman who, with all of the pain that I have endured, can still love others and forgive them. I can wrap my arms around them and say hello and mean it. It's not always easy, but the power of God helps me especially when I stop and remember grace.

Young Grasshopper

Love. I know what it is. I know how it feels.

SWNM MarQuita: Hmm...is that right?

To date I've only experienced love towards my family and some friends. Love is a hard emotion to describe, but I'll explain it the way that I see it. Love is when someone is attached to your heart. It's when a person has made such an impact on your life, that you would do almost anything for them. I love my parents, my sister, my Grandma Danzy, aunts and uncles, cousins, Godparents, friends and a lot of other people. All of them mean a lot me. Shout out to y'all!

High school seems to be the place for a lot of relationships to start. I remember attending my first school dance in the 8th grade. It was a big celebration for us, because next year we would become freshmen in high school. The dance was a lot of fun. Everyone had nice dresses and suits on to go with our theme, "Hollywood Royalty." I had on a pretty black dress that had tiny gold sparkles all over it. (Those sparkles got all over the place lol!) The food and the DJ made it even better. The night went by so fast.

I had a lot of fun dancing with my friends, however, one part of the dance (the couples dance) left me feeling a little awkward. When a slow song came on, either the few couples that were there got up to dance or friends got up to dance with one another. I wasn't a part of a couple and I didn't want to dance with my friends, so I went to the bathroom to waste time until the song was over. When it ended, we all went back to dancing together and the party became lit once again! Some of my close friends at school have been in relationships already or are currently in one. I'll tell you what it looks like to me. You like/love someone and they like/love you. Deciding to say I love you is like waiting for a ticking bomb to go off, or playing a game of who will say it first. Unfortunately, people will say I love you and won't mean it. They'll say it just to hear it said back.

From the outside looking in, relationships are cute. Sometimes I've even found myself saying, "Awe they're so cute. I want a boyfriend." *Sad face* I know relationships are a lot of work. Personally, I want to wait until I get older to be in a meaningful relationship because I feel like both the guy and I will be much more mature and will be able to handle situations more carefully than we could now. I'm not sure if my thoughts are correct but that's just what I want to do.

My mom has never been the type of parent to bring men in and out of my life. I've only met one of my mom's boyfriends (I knew she liked certain people but she only introduced me to one boyfriend) and that was only because she felt that their relationship could lead to something bigger. I guess that was a good call on mom's part because I didn't get attached to a lot of unnecessary people. My mom and I talk alot about boys, relationships, sex and things closely related to this topic. She is **VERY** blunt when she speaks, so I've heard it all I'm sure. I'm not shocked any more at the conversations we have. Mom has explained to me that she never wants me to have to find out anything from the streets and that she never wants me getting life and death information from the internet or from my friends. She explains that my body is changing and that the feelings that I have emotionally and physically are natural. God gave me these feelings and I should not hide them or be ashamed of them. She says that what I choose to *do* with these feelings is where the danger lies.

My mom and I talk about how boys my age are confused and not settled in anything (much like me at this point in my life), and that I should be careful when I start liking them so that my emotions do not run away from me and I find myself doing things that I'll later regret. She says boys will be boys. I kind of live by that quote now. LOL!

I've chosen not to be in a relationship at this point because I've seen what boys have done to my other friends. I try not to focus on boys because I need to focus on school and getting my grades and GPA up. I don't have time for them right now and that's just the truth! When the time comes I feel that I will be ready and will be in a better place to enjoy it. I'll also be waiting on having sex.

SWNM MarQuita: *Sings the Hallelujah chorus, runs 100 laps around the state of Pennsylvania, falls out, rolls on the floor, stands up, dabs and screams "Do it Lord!"*

It is my conviction based on what I believe in God's Word and in my heart to only have sex after marriage. Fornication is sex before marriage. My mom says that she wishes she would've waited, but what can you do now except not make the same mistake again? I'm sure that you can understand that I do not have much to say about this topic. I have promised to save myself until marriage. I plan to keep that promise. I was asked if I didn't keep my promise what would I do? I would repent. I know that God would forgive me as He promised. I would have to forgive myself, move on, and ask for grace and mercy to help me as I live through the consequences of my actions.

My mother and I talk about all kinds of relationships; especially friendships. First, she taught me that to have a friend I must first *be* a friend. Friends are people that you can talk to and trust. Today, I feel that people my age don't value friendship as much as I do. If you do something they don't like, it's like you're dead to them in seconds. Then, what kills me is that they'll just stop talking to you for maybe a week or two, and then all of a sudden chose to be right back to normal as if nothing has happened. That's fine. Maybe they just needed some alone time this time. But no, this is not the case. Some will do the same thing over and over and over again. This is a crazy cycle that I am guilty of being in. Once I realized what it was, I stopped it because that's not the kind of friendship that I want. It's actually not friendship at all.

I don't want friends that will be my besties one day and then turn on me the next. I want true friendship which, sadly, is rare to find. I do have a friend I feel I can count on. Sometimes we can go months without talking, but once we reconnect it's like we've never missed a beat and I love her.

Proverbs 18:24 "A man of many companions may come to ruin, but there is a friend who sticks closer than a brother."

I'm always surrounded by people, but sometimes I feel alone. Sometimes I don't feel loved.

SWNM MarQuita: I honor your feelings. Please know there is never a moment that you are not loved.

At times when I'm unhappy, it can seem like no one understands or that they don't care. (I know I'm not the only one that feels this sometimes.) My birthday is a sensitive time for me. My birthday is August 9th. It's in the middle of summer vacation. If I want to have a party or a celebration, it feels as if everyone is too busy to celebrate me. There have been many times when I cancelled birthday parties and dinners because most of the people that I wanted to be there cannot show up. It feels like the people you support can't support you. I'll admit, it hurts. I do understand that it's vacation season but I question if this is always going to be the excuse. Who knows. Usually my mom will just say reschedule, so that's what I do.

I try to get over the hurt by just thinking of other things and not really being worried about them, because my family is always there for me and I know that I am loved. I know that they appreciate me and they show it by acknowledging me and my good deeds. I'll hear "Wow that's nice. Great job." This helps me and it makes me feel good about myself, who I'm trying to be and what I'm trying to do in the world. Even though this makes me feel good, I know I can't live my life doing things just so people can acknowledge me. That's a major set up for failure and disappointment. That's putting my happiness in the hands of other people, which is something that my mom warns me against.

Since I appreciate being acknowledged, I try to show others I appreciate what they do by acknowledging them too. Thank God that He is that friend that sticks closer than a brother. He's always around. He always shows up when I need him to be there because He loves me. God's love is amazing. He created love. He is love. I feel God's love every day.

In the moments when I feel it's not there, I **KNOW** that it is just because I was allowed to wake up healthy. I know it's there because I have a roof over my head and clothes to put on my body. I am very grateful for the life God has blessed me with, the people He has placed in my life to guide me through whatever life may bring, and the opportunities He's given me. Now that love is shown to me, I can learn to show love towards other people. Thank you, God, for everything.

This is how we do it:

- **(S)** Conduct maintenance checks. In Philadelphia, we have to pay for annual emission and safety inspection checks on our cars. The emission test is to ensure that our cars are not emitting (producing or discharging) dangerous levels of pollution from their exhaust systems into the atmosphere in an effort to improve air quality. The safety inspection ensures that the cars that we are driving around in are not a safety risk for everyone on the road. Relationships need maintenance checks as well. Hey! If it's good enough for your car... Those who do not drive or do not have the responsibility for the upkeep of a car may not be able to relate to the inspection example. Here's another:

- **(S)** How do you know if the connection you have with a person is real? Check the Wi-Fi connection. If you have Wi-Fi in your home, you know it's best to link all of your electronics up to automatically connect to it while you're there. This saves on your data usage, which ultimately can save you money depending on your provider. I shared the following analogy in a sermon attempting to explain how I knew our current church was the one for us before I actually prayed about it. I would visit my new church home sporadically. I told you earlier in the book that it was states away. I thoroughly enjoyed the services. Every time I stepped into the building, all of my gifts would automatically switch on like my electronics automatically reconnects to the Wi-Fi in my home. I'd hear songs. I'd hear God speaking audibly to me. I'd hear the title of messages, and workshops. I felt God. Wi-Fi was on 1,000!! If your Wi-Fi does not go crazy around your friends, you should check your circle. You can't afford to have bad connections.

- **(S)** Expect and embrace when things come to an end. Yes, it's uncomfortable. Yes, it's unfortunate, but there will be relationships that will end. Some will end because of major conflict, and some will end because the course of your lives will take you into different directions (no harm, no foul). However it occurs, you have to be alright with the separation. We do a disservice to our growth and the growth of others when we try to hold on to the things that God and life are pulling away from us. Just because they've been there in the past doesn't mean that they will (and should) always be there. People will try to manipulate you into thinking that you've changed. You have, however, that is not always a negative thing.

Remember that change is necessary. If you are not changing you are not growing. If you do not grow you will die. Some relationships are toxic and you need to run from them at fast as humanly possible. At no time is any form of abuse (physical, mental, emotional, spiritual, etc.) appropriate or acceptable. I think I'll say it again. **AT NO TIME IS ANY FORM OF ABUSE APPROPRIATE OR ACCEPTABLE.** Honey! Do you know who you are? You are a child of the Most High God. You do not have to accept it. I don't care who its coming from. He or she is never that great or powerful for your life to be in constant danger. **GET HELP NOW.**

• **(S)** Do your part to maintain your relationships. Selfishness is not your friend. Many a relationship has been ruined because of "I, me, my." Most people will go through life with many associates (co-workers, classmates, neighbors). It takes willpower, determination, agape love, fortitude, and a good ole' dose of humility to be a friend and to have covenant relationships. Pride kills. I'd rather submit myself to the process of loving others than take a chance with no meaningful human connections. All relationships will have their highs and lows. Rest, knowing that God is a restorer. If it's in His will, any strained or broken relationship can be healed.

• **(S)** Communicate your needs in the relationship and be willing to receive the same from others. Do you know the love language of your spouse, children, siblings and friends? If your answer is no, you're already fighting a losing battle. You could be somewhere buying gifts and spending crazy amounts of money on someone who really wants kind words. Kind words from you would mean more than the price of the expensive piece of jewelry you purchased for them.

Why do we pray to God to give us exactly what we want but we make no efforts in getting to know what others want? We actually say things like, "They're going to take what I give them." Says who? That gift is probably in a corner somewhere not being used, in the trash, or better yet, has been regifted and given to someone else. You know when someone has taken the time to truly think about you before they do something for you.

The other party in the relationship also needs to know when your love tank is running low. We all get tired. We all get busy. Life pulls us in different directions. Sometimes we need someone to say, "Hey, remember me?" It's not that they are not empathetic to our needs. They just need us to stay connected and be empathetic that life is still happening to them at the same time. It's okay to ask for a date night, a family outing, a girls' day at the spa or the movies. How will anyone know the things that they are doing are well if we do not tell them? Teach people how to love you. Be willing to be taught how to love others.

- **(S)** Take time to heal.   One of the worse things that you can do post-separation is jump right back into something/someone else. You're not healed yet. You're not thinking right yet. You've simply masked the pain and will (if you're not careful) subject someone who doesn't deserve it to your uncertain process. Stop, breathe, pray, kick, scream, cry, then wipe your face and move on.

I tell you what! Niya has been there holding my hand and wiping my tears during moments when my heart was beyond broken as I have been there for her. We've also cried together when people have let us down as a unit. I've discovered that unity, even in pain, is more powerful than silent separation and seclusion. Therefore, I am not too proud to allow my child to see my tears. Something special happens here. She sees my humanity and understands that it's okay for her to be human too. She also sees the process that comes from being crushed, much like the olive. The wisdom, the understanding, the power, and the anointing that comes when we are squeezed, pushed, and pulverized is unmatched. God uses these times to process us for our next. He gets those things in us that we shouldn't have out of us. He gets those old mindsets out of us. Those old ways and habits out of us. Those old disappointments and regrets out of us. It's painful, but what it produces is promise. It humbles us so that we can be used of Him.

- **(S)** Don't fall for the okey doke! True love will never cause you to sin. Love will not ask you to lower your standards. Love will not lead you down a path of unrighteousness. Our flesh does that. As women, we naturally want to give our all to a man when we believe that we love him. Don't give him a thing until he gives you his all in the form of a ring and a promise of forever. Don't rush for that promise if it's empty words. Take your time. Let God join you to your mate. While you wait, do not allow someone to awaken a place in you when neither of you are ready. Listen to the experiences and wisdom of those who have come before you. They know what they're talking about.

- **(YG)** Boyfriends are overrated. Don't waste time focusing or loving someone who doesn't focus on loving you. You'll have to still be able to take care of and love yourself when that boy is gone, so don't count on them being your everything while they're here. At this age, you have your family or trusted guardians to meet your needs. Be grateful for this. Just focus on being better for yourself while you're young. Have fun and see the world while you're young. The time will come when you will have to take care of others. You'll be better prepared if you know who you are before that happens.

- **(YG)** Waiting until marriage to have sex is the best way to go. If you wait you don't have to worry about the person just using you for sex and you won't end up with a baby when you're not ready for one. If you actually wait, get married, and then have a baby you will have your husband and your child's father by your side. You may have also avoided having to deal with STDs (sexually transmitted diseases) if your partner waited too.

- **(YG)** Choose your friends wisely. Some will only be your friends in school. Some will only be your friends at church. That's ok. Know who they are and what role they play in your life. This helps you when you are trying to decide what you should expect from them.

- **(YG)** If ever you don't feel loved just remember the family you have by your side. If they are the ones you don't feel loved by, remember God. Think of all the good things He's done for you and thank him for His unconditional love.

*If you or anyone connected to you are in danger or are experiencing any type of abuse please call the numbers below:

The National Child Abuse Hotline 1.800.422.4453

The National Domestic Violence Hotline 1.800.799.7233 or TTY 1.800.787.3224.

RAINN Rape, Abuse, and Incest National Network 1.800.656.4673

The National Teen Dating Abuse Helpline 1.866.331.9474 or 1.866. 331 8453 (TTY)

The National Runaway Switchboard 1.800.786.2929

The National Suicide Prevention Lifeline 1.800.273. TALK (8255) (24/7 hotline) 1.888.628.9454 (Spanish) 1.800.799.4889 (TTY)

Prayer

God, we admit it. Love is a very touchy subject. A subject that's hard to master. A subject that has left many of us wounded, scarred, and discouraged. We know that this is not your fault, though we've blamed you a time or two. For this, we apologize. We know that love is not a feeling, yet we've given and received it based on what we felt in the moment. We know that love is more than words, yet we've allowed ourselves to be manipulated, fooled, disrespected, and sometimes led astray. We've also done the same to others. Forgive us. We apologize for defining things that are not found within your character as love. We chose to be led by our own lust and desires. God, we've been crushed during those times where we while operating in integrity towards others experienced our love, friendship and companionship abused and disregarded. We need to heal. We've expected humans to love as you. We've expected our parents to be perfect and love as you. We've expected our spouses and our children to be perfect and love as you. We've expected our leaders, family and friends to be who they say that they are and love as you. When they failed us, we've failed you. Forgive us. Father we know that **YOU** are love. You are love that loved so much that you gave love (yourself). Your love is eternal. It goes from everlasting to everlasting. It never gives up on us. It never waivers. Your love is consistent and it's accountable. Please help us to love others as you have loved us. Help us to show your love to a dying world. Help us to be the friend to others that you have been to us. Help us to forgive others as you have forgiven us. You've been an amazing model for us to follow. We appreciate you.

In Jesus name we pray, Amen

8

God Gave You Life—LIVE!

Green Bean

There's a beautiful timeless song that speaks to how cold it must be living in another's shadow. I've had to sing it many times in various professional venues. One day while preparing for a performance, I took the time to really think about the words that I had grown so accustomed to singing. For whatever reason, they hit me like a ton of bricks. I remember saying to myself "Wow. The writer makes such a powerful statement in the first line. It's a source of so many problems. We should never live in anyone's shadow."

There's also a problem with following in the footsteps of someone else, too. The Bible in **Psalm 37:23-24** declares that, "The steps of a man are established by the Lord, when he delights in his way; though he fall, he shall not be cast headlong (carelessly, recklessly, in a rush) for the Lord upholds his hand." The Lord God should be the **only** person establishing (setting up, organizing, making the rules for) our steps. I understand that we want to keep the family traditions. I understand that we want to honor the wishes of those we feel have sacrificed so much for us to get to a certain point. There's nothing wrong with that. There's nothing wrong with using the wisdom and guidance of your support system. They are watching out for you. They want to keep you safe.

As you mature (and can handle all of the responsibilities that come along with maturing), you realize a few things. If God has spoken to them, giving them instruction and direction for their lives, He most certainly can and will do the same for you. Your life, though it may have similarities in certain areas with others, was never meant to be lived the same way. You cannot allow that unnecessary pressure to consume your thoughts. If you live in fear that your decisions to walk the path that God has laid out for you will disappoint everyone else, you'll disappoint the most important person - **YOU**. Oh, I like this one! You realize that if God desired for you to live under someone else's shadow, He would have never given you your own. Truth is, the only shadow you should abide under is the shadow of the Almighty. **(Psalm 91:1)**

SWNM Niya: Preach, preacher!

SWNM MarQuita: Put me in F sharp please!

I've been extremely careful in this particular area with my daughter. The first things that she normally hears when people meet us either collectively for the first time or when I'm introducing her to people that I know for the first time is, "Oh my goodness, that is your twin!" "Niya you look **EXACTLY** like your mother!" "She spit you out!" The next question to usually follow, especially when those people know what I do in ministry is, "Do you sing like your mother?" I could see that Niya, at times, was bothered by this.

It must be confusing to hear, "Niya, don't be like me, don't act like me, don't live like me, don't walk like me" from your mother but hear, "You look *just* like your mom, you sound *just* like your mom, you smile *just* like your mom, do you sing *just* like your mom" as soon as you're in the public. I've always been aware that if I don't build her up to be secure in herself, these comparisons could potentially harm her at a very pivotal time in her life where she is searching for her own identity. I used to jump in before she could answer and reply, "No, Niya is Niya. She tried to steal my face, but she's her own person. She acts like Niya.

She sings like Niya." Then I'd go on to describe the range and tone of her voice (which I absolutely adore).

It was my way of saving the day in the moment. I never wanted her to compare herself to me. I never wanted her to feel that she had to do what I do. I never wanted her to feel that she had to explain why we were different. We're supposed to be. At this stage in her life Niya is finding within herself the unique qualities that makes her a designer's original. She's finding her voice, her song, her purpose and enjoying what I like to call selective independence (Yup. I'm making history here coining phrases and supplying definitions and stuff! LOL). Selective independence is when a teenager *chooses* between reverting back to being a small helpless child with all of the benefits that came along with it, finding peace with the limitations given to them based on their chronological age and governing themselves accordingly, or losing their minds by way of testing limits and trying to live a much older and more independent life than they're ready for.

We *know* that the people who make the comments and ask the questions of her are absolutely pure in intention and we *know* it comes from a beautiful place. I've processed this with Niya. In processing, I realized that I had done the same thing to other people without thinking about it myself! It's just one of the ways that our human minds "connect the dots." It's a way that we make sense of things. God can allow two different people to have so many similarities that it is simply amazing! I get it! To be honest, I'm totally honored that God allowed the offspring to look like me. I mean, hello! Do you know how many times she hears, "You are **GORGEOUS**?" Deductive reasoning causes me to conclude that if she's gorgeous, and she looks just like me, then I, I must be gorgeous, right? Right! Vanity! All is vanity! LOL! I'll take it, and I don't feel no ways tired about it! LOL!

I was born into a family full of preachers and pastors. My mother is a pastor. My mother never pressured me to follow in her footsteps in anyway. Now, she most certainly had expectations, but I didn't go through life feeling like I had to be just like her. I think she knew that was not going to happen anyway! LOL! My brother and I grew up watching our mother continue her education and certifications, being involved in her business ventures, and the ministry. She has never been a slacker. A boss indeed.

Naturally, I followed suit in wanting to have my own, wanting to be successful, and wanting to be someone that my daughter could look up to, but I did not follow in her exact footsteps. For one, The Dukes shoes are way too big for me to fill so I'm not even trying to. Secondly, we are two totally different people. I want my daughter to feel the same about me. I want to be a point of reference but not the reference point. There is a difference. A point of reference is a person place or thing that is part of a larger plan, a larger scope, a larger conversation. A point of reference can be included in a list of things you can choose from based on what you've been exposed to. For example: When it's time for my daughter to build her first home, she can use the years of watching me change, restructure, and rebuild ours as a point of reference. Since our home is not the only home that she's seen, she can use what she admires from other homes as well. A reference point is the standard for comparison, the basis for evaluations. It is the criteria.

Whoa. I am in no way so great that my daughter's entire life has to be based off of who I am and what I've done. Not at all. Again, my prayers for her is that she is so much better than I could ever imagine being and that she doesn't make any of the mistakes I've made or anything worse. I want her to dream and not be afraid of dreaming. I want her to soar and not be afraid of the fall. I want her to laugh as loudly as she wants to, and smile as bright as the sun. I want her to love who she sees when she looks at herself in the mirror. I want her to see the beauty in everything that God created and never allow anyone or anything to dim the eternal light that He has given her. She will never be free to live her life comparing her life to mine. I share with her that I will ALWAYS have her back. I'll always be there for her. Period.

Living your life can be scary! You're sure to make mistakes. If we make them as adults, our children most certainly will. That's alright. I'll defend her even in those. I'll correct her when necessary, but defend her. Parents, I believe that it is extremely important for your children to see you openly defend them. Defend their right to be free. Defend their right to be different. Defend their right to be respected. Defend their right to grow up.

I remember when Niya was little. Her eyes used to resemble the shape of eyes that we would normally associate with another ethnicity. A nickname was given to her because of it. Niya hated it. It really bothered her. When she came to me and told me that she did not like people calling her that, I went to those people and shared her sentiment. Everyone stopped calling her the nickname except one person. She totally disregarded my child's feelings and made it a point in that moment to call her the name again openly so that my child could hear it. At that point, I made it a point to make a point. I looked this woman in her eyes and told her that she would not call my daughter out of her name again, and if she did, I would proceed to call her out of hers. Needless to say, we never heard that term again.

Deep down inside (waaaaaaayyyyyy deep) I knew that that woman didn't mean my child any harm, but her actions were causing harm. She thought her age and status would give her the green light to say something to my child that I asked her not to. No ma'am. You do not have that authority. I am accountable for her life at this point. I will defend it at all cost. (Follow me as I follow Christ...not sure if this qualifies as being led by the spirit. This is more being led by the momma lioness ready to pounce at a second's notice tendencies that I have especially when it comes to my child).

I believe it is equally important for your children to see you choosing to be humble. When you give others a place of authority in their lives, you will, at times, have to take a cautious back seat. I would like to use my mom as an example because she has automatic authority to chastise and correct my child, however, she's such a softy with her grandchildren that it's a moot point. I mean these grands of hers get away with murder compared to what we got in trouble for growing up! (Bro. Ray and Sis. Lauren, can I get an Amen? Thank ya.)

SWNM Niya: *That is not true!*

SWNM MarQuita: *It's as true as true can be!*

We must teach our children how to listen and respect other adults who are not related to them. We must teach our children how to be a leader who knows how to follow. I love to learn. When I can sit back, follow someone else's lead and learn something from them in an area that they shine in, I'm in heaven! Their passion draws me in and I am inspired. A good leader knows that there will be times where they'll have to step up and say, "Hey, this is what we're going to do." Then there are times when they'll have to depend on someone else or defer to someone else to instruct them with, "This is what you need to do." Humility gives us the grace to honor others whether we are leading them or not.

There are many pitfalls that I try to teach Niya to avoid. Among them are fear, doubt, who and they. I've seen the word "fear" broken down into so many acronyms. One in particular that I've addressed in the past is that fear stands for "false evidence appearing real." I get the concept. At the same time, I believe it's pretty damaging when used out of context. The evidence is only false when it's not true. That's not always the case. There are some real things that we are absolutely afraid of. The feelings are real, the anxiety is real, the power that thing has to cripple us is real. We've witnessed (seen the evidence) of what it's done to people in a very real way.

Fact is, the God we serve is greater, so we in His might, tap into the power He gives us to overcome. When we downplay the power of our enemy, we place ourselves in a place of dangerous vulnerability. I cringe when I hear people say that Satan is not powerful. I don't get why anyone would say things like, "He's stupid." I'm sorry? Have you not read your Bible? He's so stupid that he knows how to walk the earth, and how to make accusations about us to God after he's watched us in order to present us with the exact things he knows will knock us off of our square. He's so unintelligent that his organized kingdom does not stand divided. Yeah ok. Listen, fear is real. It's a mind killer. We just have the greatest power dwelling on the inside of us to combat it.

Doubt is a form of fear. It's a lack of confidence or uncertainty. Doubt normally comes from listening to the wrong voices (internally/externally). Those voices are normally attached to a *who* or a *they*. I've told Niya not to come to me with what *they* said. *Who* are *they*? Experience has shown that most times when someone inserts a "*they* told/asked me" "or *they* said" in a story, it's a lie. I'm not big on secret squirrel sagas. Drop names please. God told Adam to name the animals. Jesus asked the disciples, "*Who* do you and men say that I am?" When operating in spiritual warfare, you identify the spirit by its name. In life, you need to be able to identify your goals and your obstacles so you'll know how to attain them/overcome them. Let's operate in the specifics.

The *whos* and *theys* are intimidating so many powerful people. Quick example. You are afraid to fly. Why? You received some bit of information about flying that made you uncomfortable. Well *who* created or gave you the information? What did *they* say? Are *they* credible? Are *they* operating out of a place of fear and you've willingly taken on their feelings, or are *they* so caught up on being better than you that *they* will never support you flying because *they* know once you get a taste of being in the air, you will soar! Is it jealousy? *Who* told you that this is the only experience to choose to listen to? Have *they* given you their advice because no one has ever done what you will do so there is no point of reference? *Who* said that God didn't create you to be the reference point? Beloved, *who* told you the sky's the limit? *Who* told you you weren't good enough, pretty enough, fast enough? *Who* told you that you would never be allowed to stand on platforms? *Who* told them that their platforms were good enough for you to stand on?

I can really go on, but I think you get the point. Too often we allow other people's thoughts of us based on their life experiences to dictate *who* we are and what we will become but *they*, like Satan, are liars. I told you in earlier chapters that I've never been one to listen much to other people's nonsense, so I asked the Lord to give me a creative way to show Niya how limitless she really is - and He did. One day driving in the car, I asked her a simple question. I said "Niya, what is our home address?" She answered. "Our home is in what part of the city?" She answered again. I continued. This part of the city is found in the city of? This city is a part of what state? This state is a part of what country? What coast of the country? This country is on what continent? *Who* owns these continents? *Who* owns the bodies of water that surround the continents? YOUR GOD! Sooooooo...why can't you and *who* said it? Irrelevant. Girl, you were created to change the world! *Who*? You!

It has always been and will always remain paramount for me to expose my daughter to things beyond what I've been blessed to see or experience (and I've been blessed to see and experience a lot.) There's a great big world out there waiting to be inspired by what God has deposited within her. Her life was given to her to change nations. It's not cliché. It's true. She saved me.

*SWNM Niya: *FLIPS hair with my cape blowing in the wind behind me**

Each life that I've been blessed to reach blesses others. As that reach expands, nations are blessed all because of her. I've taught Niya that the love she needs, the strength she needs, the discipline that she needs starts within the four walls of our home. It then spreads to our immediate community, but it cannot stop there. If she never goes beyond the mentality of our home, or the culture of our immediate community how can she change the world? So we must go to the world. We will stand on every continent. My prayer is that with a view of the world, Niya will make world changing decisions. With a world view the desire to fulfill temporary pleasures, the awkwardness and peer pressure that comes along with being a teenager hopefully won't affect her as much.

World changers can't get lost in insignificant things. I teach Niya not to major in the minors. I remind her to stay focused. Be aware of the distractions and the attacks of the enemy that will seem to come out of nowhere. The attacks have a purpose that's why your prayers must have purpose. I teach her not to waste time going tit for tat. My mother would say, "You kill my dog, I kill your cat." Why bother? We all will reap what we sow. Let God handle those situations as they come. Speaking of handling things, I teach Niya that if she's handling business, do it right. Render every service that you give as if you are giving it to the Lord. Keep your word. Be on time. Research your clients or potential business partners before you enter into a contract. Never sign your name on anything without thoroughly weighing the pros and cons. Asks all of the questions you need to. If you are not in agreement, don't feel pressured or manipulated in signing it. What you need to see about a person is normally revealed when they feel questioned or antagonized. You're not antagonizing them. You're smart enough to know your own value.

Remember that you don't owe anyone anything because they feel they've opened a door for you. You don't have to have sex with them to get ahead. (They themselves are trying to get ahead. Don't be fooled.) You don't have to become their yes girl, become their flunky, or anything else. Be thankful, be grateful, pay it forward, but do not become a slave to them. There is no such thing as family and friend benefits when conducting business. Never be afraid to ask for what you are worth and hold people accountable to their word to you. Trust that if the shoe was on the other foot they surely would nickel and dime you for what they need.

You can't loan everyone money. When you do loan it out, it's okay to want your money back. Keep other people from behind the wheel of your car. I don't care how badly they need it. If something should happen to them in your car, you are responsible for it and them. Don't be moved when people threaten or attempt to assassinate your character with words or in deed because you did not do or respond to them in a way that they wanted. People will lie on you. If you have done what they said, okay. If you've repented, it's under the blood. Let them talk. Let them share secrets. YOU move on. Don't lose a wink of sleep over it. God's got that, honey. Sit back and watch Him work.

Build your resume. Seek positive experiences that will lead you down the road to success. Don't be afraid to fail. Failure is inevitable, but so is the victory. In those moments where you do fail, Jesus must be at the root of your recovery. Bounce back taking things one step at a time. The time it takes you to reach a goal is not always as important as you actually reaching the goal. Get out of your own way. Let God make you great.

It's okay to stand up for what you believe and speak up against what you feel is unjust. It's okay to take the unpopular stance. It's okay to go against the machine when the machine is wicked. Speak up for yourself. Stand your ground. You have the authority. With Jesus, you are a powerful light all by yourself. The only person that has the power to make you feel small is you. I don't care who they **THINK** they are, **KNOW** who you are.

At the same time, remember that your journey does not make you better than anyone, and that you cannot make this journey through life alone. We need each other. Be sensitive to those moments when God tells you to sow into someone, a business, or a dream. Listen when He tells you not to charge or to give the honorarium back. Do it without looking for any recognition. Do it without looking for any praise. Be okay with saying **NO**. Be okay with taking a break. Take a vacation and actually vacate. My mother always said, "One monkey doesn't stop the show." Things will still move on whether you are there or not. If you've done your job as a good leader (should you be in a leadership position), things should move better because you've trained those running with the baton to be better than you.

I promise you, our mission is living. If anyone should ask you where are the Danzy Divas you tell them, "Somewhere having fun, living and giving God glory." Did you read that? Having FUN. If you haven't heard or read these words before, let me be the first to share them with you: It's okay to relax. It's okay to take a break. It's okay to yell and scream in excitement. I believe that every once in awhile, you should treat your lungs to a hardy laugh. I mean a laugh from your gut. I am in no way a doctor, but it seems to me that a good slap your knee laugh should be good for your insides somewhere.

We need moments where we can clear our hearts and minds from the business of our daily responsibilities. I've made a declaration that when it's all said and done besides hearing, "Well done thy good and faithful servant", I want to be able to look at Niya's life and my life and say, "You've done good girls, you've done good!"

Our home is full of joy and laughter, much like the home I grew up in. If we're not laughing at a show, or something that we've found online, we are most certainly laughing at ourselves and absolutely laughing at one another. It's what we do for laughter is good for the soul. I find joy in the other relationships in my life. My friends are hilarious. My coworkers are hilarious. The strangers I meet, hilarious! Maybe hilarity just follows me! Now that I think about it, humor is like an unwritten prerequisite for friendship with me. Friend equals crazy, touched, hilarious. Go figure. Laughter definitely helps in a house with two developing Divas.

My daughter is very direct and outspoken, but extremely laid back with this honest, sarcastic, dry humor. That can be a recipe for disaster when you're dealing with a mom who's pretty much on top of everything all of the time. (Some may call it being "controlling." I call it being "me." Hush now.) We've had to learn how to do things to cut the tension. I actually enjoy this little thing that Niya does in response to a directive where she squares her shoulders and says, "Fight me. Swing first mom." (Please note that this only happens when we are both clear that we are playing and in a safe place to laugh. Trust, she knows when Mom is not there.)

When Niya was younger, we use to play rock paper scissors when it was time to divide the workload or to prove who may have been right or wrong in a situation. We have our own nonverbal language. This helps when the words of our mouths and the meditations of our hearts will most certainly NOT be acceptable in God's sight. The dynamic is quite interesting to see. It may not work for everyone, but it works for us. It has taught us tolerance and has eliminated situations from blowing up. When we mess up, we deal with it. We reason together. At some point in our reasoning, we find ourselves laughing (well, most of the time).

I want to create lasting memories with and for my child. I try to make everything (even those things that may seem blah and uneventful) as extraordinary as possible. Niya had no choice but to become my travel buddy as I went to the cities, states, and now countries to minister. I wanted her to walk through every door that God allowed me to walk through. It is my responsibility to expose her to "more." I loved watching her sleep on those long flights to Cali. I did not like waking up to the hundreds of pictures she snapped of me sleeping on those long flights to Cali (but it's precious nonetheless.) I loved watching her look out of the window in amazement at the beautiful scenery as we drove up to New York. I loved the little songs she made up and the restroom shenanigans that she created as we drove back and forth to Ohio. I loved how she would try to stay up to keep me company as we traveled back and forth to Harrisburg. Parents, you want to learn things about your children? Take a long car ride. You can learn a lot in those three to seven hours. We talked about everything from school, boys, music, the necessity for a spike in her allowance (nice try), church, and family.

SWNM Niya: *It was worth a shot!*

I love embarrassing her at the red lights. I pull up next to unsuspecting cars on the road with the windows down, music blasting, attempting to do the new dances and singing off key. It blesses me! LOL! The sporadic challenges and dance offs that occur in our home are priceless! If we saw a carnival, we went. The museums and the zoo? On it! At times when we were not on the road, we made "staycations" just as fun. We stayed in our home eating takeout and ordering movies. We went to a hotel for a weekend where we enjoyed going swimming, shopping, and challenging ourselves to eat at safe (yet unfamiliar) places, pushing ourselves beyond our limits of "normal."

You want purple hair? Try it! You want to go ziplining? Let's do it! Life's for living – with no regrets. Now that she's older and more independent, I've had to take a step back and let her make some of her memories with her friends. I supply the cash, the rules of conduct and the time to be home. She's wise enough to know that she must comply if she wants to retain the freedom she desires. Niya and I have even started writing our bucket list together. Some things we will do together, others we will not.

The process of thinking ahead has been eye opening for me. I gain greater insight to who she is becoming, and I must say that I am so proud. I can't wait to take our relationship to another level and have the adult adventures. The greatest part of the adult adventures is that she will then be fully responsible for her way there, whatever money she will choose to spend while there, and everything in between. What's more is that at this point in our relationship, she'll be able to take care of ME! (Can the church shout yeah?!) Parents, understand that you cannot wait until your child reaches this level of maturity to lay the foundation of desiring to spend time with one another. At 15, my child still climbs in the bed with me, snuggles up next to my cheek and snores. We still do our "I want to cuddle" thing that we do. Nope. Her breath is not as cute as it used to be, but it's hers nonetheless. I pop a mint in it when I can, making sure she won't choke on it, or simply turn my face away. Just knowing she's there next to me willingly does my heart so much joy. I wouldn't want it any other way.

In our home, we have dedicated walls for writing our thoughts individually and for each other. You will find inspirational words are all over the place. My brother shakes his head when he's over and says, "You're just like your momma!" I guess I am slowly but surely turning into a Mini Diva Duke. LOL! We love to DIY (do it yourself). Our home is our own art gallery full of things we've created like picture frames made into mirrors, art made from yarn and felt, and beautifully painted canvases. We take old things, rip them, bleach them, and then sew them into new pieces, and they're nice. In the past, we've made nice accessories that were actually sold to others! In my basement are organized bins of glue and glitter, fabric, needle and thread, yarn, paint, gardening tools (yes, we love to garden). You name it. We are always ready when inspiration hits us. I like when inspiration hits us.

We even have a special way that we say "I love you" to one another. It is a must that we say good morning and goodnight to one another before we go to bed. One night, Niya came into my room and said, "Mom, I think I'm going to bed. I'm tired." She bent down to kiss me and said, "Goodnight." I responded "Goodnight Niya, I love you." She said, "I love you too." I continued by saying, "Always and forever." She looked at me and smiled and replied, "Always and forever." It became settled in the heavens in that moment. We say it whenever we part ways be it for an hour, a day, a week, from a phone conversation, it doesn't matter. Whenever we part, we remind each other that, "I love you, always and forever." Truth is, you never know when the last time is the last time. I always want my daughter to know that I'll love her beyond my life.

There's a strand of selfishness inside of me that wants to scream "**NO!** Don't grow up. Don't leave me. Don't start looking like that or maturing in that way. Don't start asking those questions or become interested in that." But alas (I'm being very dramatic here. You can't see me, but trust that I am), it's happening whether I want it to or not. I want to be able to protect her every second of everyday by keeping her stapled to my hip but that's unrealistic, and it will only harm her in the long run. I'll take what time I have left and make the best of it. I absolutely love walking into her room while she's asleep and kissing the apples of her cheeks. I love when she sneaks into my room and jumps on my bed or climbs into my bed to talk or sleep. I love watching her explore new hairstyles and practice her makeup in the mirror in her room. I love our goofy, comical, extemporaneous skits and dances. I question that she'll still want to call me and talk to me every day when she leaves.

Are these moments only happening now because she's here? Is she still going to find the peace in crawling into my bed when she visits me on break from college, or even after she's married (if that is God's will)? Is she still going to be my travel buddy? I sure hope so. I'll miss her (I'm crying now) as these are some of my most cherished moments as her mommy.

Turns to face my daughter SWNM Niya: *Mom, are you about to cry?*

SWNM MarQuita: *Yes. Yes I am.*

Niya, **YOU** are the reason why I work so hard. **YOU** are worth every sacrifice. **YOU** are the reason why I've taken some of the hits that I have endured in life. **YOU** are the reason why I save. Know that I must stress the importance of an education. I must correct you, chastise you, and say no to you at times. I owe you transparency. That's why I share the ups and downs, the good bad and ugly of my life. **I LOVE YOU**, and my love will last **FOREVER**. (Ok, I'm crying again.) I don't know where I'd be today if God hadn't allowed you to come when you did. I'm sure it wouldn't be writing this book in an effort to inspire, educate, support, uplift and challenge other parent/child relationships. I'm sure of that. Remember that you live, you die, and then you're judged. Respect the time given to you. Live a life that will produce limited regrets. Never forget that the moments in between your dash must be authentic to your purpose on this earth *Attempts to dry my face*

I love how Solomon ends the book of **Ecclesiastes** in **Chapter 12**. He starts verse 13 off by writing, "The end of the matter; all has been heard." In other words, that's it, I'm done! LOL! He continues to write **Ecclesiastes 12:13** "...Fear God and keep His commandments, for this is the whole duty of man." What else is there to say? Live so that God can be pleased. It is after all, your responsibility.

Sweet Pea

My mom says life can be hard. She says there are a lot of ups and downs and that it's okay to mess up as long as you get up. She doesn't want me to be afraid to try new things. Mom says that it's okay to try things and figure out if you like them or not rather than not trying them at all. (She's talking about good, clean, safe things of course.)

You'll never become the person you're supposed to be if you are afraid of change, even if it's changing small things like a new lipstick color. In the end, it's the little things that make our lives different from everyone else. My mom tells me not to worry about what everyone else is doing but to make sure that what I'm doing is good. She says to make sure that I keep God with me at all times, and to have faith that He will supply all of my needs. My mom wants to be able to trust me to go out and live, but live responsibly.

If I had a quarter for every time someone said I looked like my mom, I'd be a millionaire. I know that people say it because honestly, we do look alike. I just don't want people to see me as "MarQuita." I want to be seen as Niya. The comments are cool, but when people expect me to **be** like my mom, this is where it becomes a problem.

For example, I'm asked, "Do you sing like your mom?" No. Sorry. I don't sing like my mom. I sing like myself. My mom says that she loves the range and tone of my voice, and she doesn't want me to be like her at all. She says she wants me to be better. She understood that it sometimes bothered me when people asked if I sang like her when I was younger, so she'd usually comment before I did. (Thanks mom). Now that I'm older she's stepping back a little. I'm sure there will be times when I'm not with her and people will ask me the same questions, so I have to be ready. Mom taught me to stand up for myself but still be respectful. I can simply just say, "No, but I do sing." This way, I am still respectful to whoever is asking but also answering the question.

I'm becoming my own person. Sooner or later, I'll have to start taking care of myself, but for now I'm enjoying sitting back with the little responsibility that I do have while having fun, fun, fun! I'll miss being able to sleep in all day. I'll miss not having to pay for things. Most of all, I'll miss the security of depending on my parents. Although I'll miss being able to do some things I'm looking forward to new adventures. I'm looking forward to driving so I can go where I want. I am mostly excited about owning my own home, because I want to decorate it the way that I want it to look.

Ecclesiastes 2:24 reads, "There is nothing better for a man, than that he should eat and drink, and that he should make his soul enjoy good in his labour. This also I saw, that it was from the hand of God." My mom and I have a lot of fun when we hang out. She says if you work hard, you should be able to play hard.

We do a lot of activities together. We ice skate, roller skate, paint pottery, garden, cook, go to the movies, Broadway and stage plays, to the beach, shop and travel. With all of that time spent between the two of us, we have a lot of time to bond. The activities we do are already fun but when you have someone that you can talk to openly, it makes the experience even better. I've always liked the fact that I can talk to mom about almost anything. When we go shopping sometimes, we might pick up the same thing because our styles are similar. Our love for clothing is something we bond over. Mom likes to shop a lot! We even shop at consignment and second-hand stores. She always finds the good stuff. I don't, which makes my experience not as great as hers. I'm still okay with it because we're together. Some days if I'm blessed enough I'll find a couple of good pieces. Good pieces equal more clothes!

Truthfully, I love hanging out with my mom. We don't have to go anywhere. We can just chill. Sometimes we will watch movies and eat all day. Mom tries to make sure that it's a balance between the healthy foods that we eat and the not-so-healthy things we both love like super greasy pepperoni pizza! I like staying in the house more than going out at times because when you go out (especially with my mother), you have to make sure you look 100% presentable. When it's just us, she's okay with whatever I wear. During these times, we share with each other things that we like or talk about things that are going on in our lives. These are the best times to me.

I consider my mom and I to be pretty creative people. Creating new things with her takes excitement to another level. We've recycled old clothing in the past. We've even attempted to make items of our own with an idea, new fabric and a sewing machine. Mom and I do a lot of arts and crafts (not only paper and glue arts and crafts, but big things.)

She, my God Mom Lynnette, and bonus Grandma Delores Yancy are the main people that inspired me into wanting to create my own accessories instead of just buying them. I remember one day, my mom and I were in a store and I asked her to buy me a pair of sparkly blue sunglasses. My mom looked at the price tag and said, "For eight dollars? Oh no, we can make these at home!" It was true! So true in fact that I started making my own jewelry at the age of 10 or 11. Rubber band bracelets were my thing! I would make them nice and neat. I could also make them fast. It never took me more than three minutes to finish a regular bracelet. My mom told me that they were really good and that she wanted one too. Having the hustler spirit that I have, I came up with the idea to start selling them.

SWNM MarQuita: I'm sorry. Hustler spirit? What's a hustler? Who is the author and finisher of such a spirit?

SWNM Niya: Mom!

Teenagers, you can do this also. It's never too late to do something that you love. Initially, I made plain bracelets with nothing on them, but then I started to add charms and letters. The bracelets would sell out. My taste changed. I stopped making rubber band bracelets and started making regular bracelets. Those bracelets sold as well, but I got bored again and stopped. I still make them but I don't sell them anymore. I was at an age where my mom said it was okay for me to start and stop some things until I found out what I really wanted to focus on. She helped me manage everything with my business to make sure that it all went well.

During this process, I learned that mothers and daughters can have fun when there is a common goal of success in mind. We really had a lot of fun together. I even tried to teach her how to make her own rubber bracelets (which she failed at). She said my job was to make them and her job was to keep me motivated. She really brought it all together. #ThankYouMom

Music is a big part of my life. I was in the studio the entire time my mom recorded her EP. I've traveled all across the U.S. because my mom sings. I've been able to stand on my own stages because of my participation in concert choirs and sing in some pretty cool venues. I have been in multiple school musicals. My mom has been my biggest cheerleader at every event.

I'm surrounded by music 24/7 and I love it. I listen to music to relieve myself from the pressure surrounding me. It definitely makes me feel better. Did you know that scientist believe that music can detect the kind of mood you are in? If ever you feel stressed out just turn up your favorite song and dance in the mirror and go crazy. Why not? After all who really doesn't like music? It's fun to listen to and will most definitely be around forever. I love when my mom and I have little dance offs when a good song comes on, or when she hears about a popular dance and wants me to teach it to her (which she fails at again).

SWNM MarQuita: *I don't know what you're talking about. I can dance! LOL!*

I mean, at least she's not afraid to try or look silly in my eyes. That's what I love about her. My mom shows me that when you love someone, you should be willing to let your hair down and be free to love them and laugh with them in the moment. We have a lot of these moments. I'm so glad that we do.

This is how we do it:

- **(GB)** Always remember Jesus. We should never believe that we have done any great thing within ourselves. We should always strive to have grateful hearts. Entitlement fortifies a prideful spirit. Entitlement gives you a false sense of who you really are and what you really deserve. Truth is that we are dust. We are sinners. We deserve to die. But God!

- **(GB)** Give each other space to live and go along for the ride. Parents you cannot control your children's lives. Since we're talking about riding, let's use a car for this analogy.

  You teach them about the importance of balancing the wheels of their drive and motivation. Every life must have balance. You teach them to align their lives with the will of God so the weight of who they are and will become is evenly distributed. You teach them the importance of regular oil changes (check your oil naturally and spiritually). You encourage them to carry proper insurance, i.e. coverage. They need someone watching over them. But then you sit back as they grab the keys, you buckle your seatbelt and you pray. You pray they allow you in the car and that those moments are the best moments ever. Point out the beauty at every pit stop. Have fun.

- **(GB)** Don't let people discourage your creativity in life. You were born for a purpose, so don't let human opinions alter the real you. Parents, make it a rule in your home that you will always create space for the span of your children's wings. While having fun, remind each other that your lives are for a greater purpose. There is a responsibility to the call.

- **(GB)** Try to make the things that may not be fun, fun (i.e. chores, school work, writing this book, lol!) If you are music lovers, blast the music while you work. Dance! Give prizes to the person who complete their tasks first. Invite others to help you with promise of pizza after they're done. Never let the fun out of the fun things, even if it becomes lucrative.

- **(GB)** Document the moments.   Take lot of pics. Journal. Create memories that will last beyond your lifetime.

- **(GB)** Get a passport and travel the world!   This is pretty self-explanatory. Get the passport. Use the passport. Renew the passport. Repeat. You'll be happy that you did!

- **(SP)** Life is coming, so just brace yourself.   There's nothing you can do to stop it. Just enjoy the ride. Make sure to stay with God and stay humble. With God taking the ride with you how could you ever get lost?

- **(SP)** Parents, don't be afraid to try new things with your children or teens with your parents. My mom and I went back to seriously gardening in the summer of 2017 and it was so therapeutic for us. We never thought that that is what we would've done, but we did it and it's been amazing. We love to garden and take care of the yard now and it also gives us more time to spend together.

- **(SP)** Make sure to always be yourself.   Do what makes you happy whether that is singing, dancing or whatever! Make sure you're having fun. Life is not guaranteed forever so you want to make the best of the moments that you have. Spend time with family and friends and just live life because God gave one to ya!

Prayer

Lord you made us from the dust of the earth. You breathed the breath of life into us, and we became living souls. Our purpose is to serve you, love you, obey you and lead more souls to you. We want to hear you say "well done" when our time on earth has passed. Help us to live a life that's pleasing to you. We need you in order to please you. Give us the boldness to settle into *our* purpose within our families, in our circle of friendships, in our churches, our communities and in the Kingdom. No one can be us but us. No one can accomplish our task on earth but us. We are significant. We are your handiwork and we are good. Help us to see the importance of fulfilling our destiny while we have the strength and the ability to do so. We make this request - keep us from being anxious. Help us to pray, make our petitions known, and to thank you in everything. Then and only then will this journey with all of its ups and downs be worth it. We will find ourselves revived and refreshed by the peace you give us. It exceeds and goes beyond our understanding. While we're here God, we know that you intend for us to experience the beauty of your creation. Give us a desire to truly live as you have given us the ability to build, to learn, and to have fun. It is an insult to you for us to isolate our thoughts, our experiences, and ourselves from you and from others. Let us be bold enough to live and laugh out loud! Remove the fear of failure from our spirits. We limit you when we limit ourselves. When it's time, teach us how to rest as you rested. Teach us how to sit back and look at what you've allowed us to create and accomplish to be able to say that it is good. Teach us to be inspired by the smallest things and help us to be the inspiration for others. We thank you for every blessing. We thank you for every door. We thank you for allowing us the opportunity to *do this life thing together*. Now keep us together. Keep us united. Keep us in peace and support of one another. Keep the love that we have for one another flowing from heart to heart. Keep the respect that we have and the laughter that we have real and authentic. Let us continue to be each other's safe place. Thank you for matching our souls up for the journey. The lessons we are learning from one another are invaluable. The times we are sharing together are priceless. Godly parents are a manifestation of your love on earth and our children are our reward. We are excited about what you have in store for us. You have the steering wheel and we're along for the ride. Our lives are yours. We trust you and we are safe.

In Jesus name we pray, Amen.

MarQuita: *Standing up to offer you final refreshments* *We've enjoyed our time with you. I pray this is just the beginning of more great conversations to come. Niya say goodbye to our guests.*

Niya: *With a smile this time* *Bye! **Picks up cell phone as all teenagers do, and walks away. ***

Printed in the United States
By Bookmasters